Finding Myron
an adopted son's search for his birth father

Reginald D. Jarrell

BLUE
CEDAR
PRESS

Blue Cedar Press
Wichita, Kansas

Blue Cedar Press
PO Box 48715
Wichita, KS 67201

Visit the Blue Cedar Press website: www.bluecedarpress.com
10 9 8 7 6 5 4 3 2 1
First edition February 2024

ISBN 978-1-958728-16-1 (paper)
ISBN 978-1-958728-17-8 (ebook)

Cover and interior design by Gina Laiso, Integrita Productions
Editors Laura Tillem and Gretchen Eick

Library of Congress Control Number: 2023949737

Printed in the United States of America at IngramSpark.

Dedication

For my two mothers,
Wanda Louise McClain-Grant and Ellen Jarrell,
my two fathers,
Fred Jarrell and Myron Clay II,
and the mother of my children,
Canetha S. Jarrell, with love across eternity.

CONTENTS

INTRODUCTION

I was about to make the phone call that would lead to the discovery of "who" I was.

On a crisp but clear Saturday night in October 2009, I sat in a rental car in a Kansas City, Missouri suburb about one block from my biological father's duplex. I was about to meet this man, face to face, after fifty plus years of questions, doubts, and dreams. This is the story of my search and discovery of my father.

The backstory:

In 1956, Wanda Louise McClain was 13 years old, and pregnant by a neighborhood boy two years older. Wanda lived with her mother, Rosie Lee, and stepfather, Bernard Wilson, in a house in central Kansas City, Missouri. Other children in the household were Wanda's younger half-sister Rosetta, aka Pee Wee, whose father's name I never learned, and Denise, her half-sister by Rosie Lee's marriage to Bernard. Rosie Lee was also pregnant at this time. Her baby, Oggerita, would be born after her daughter Wanda's. There was constant friction between Rosie Lee's three daughters and Bernard and no room for another baby. Wanda was sent to live in an unwed mothers' facility operated by a local Catholic church where several nuns pressured her to place her baby for adoption. Wanda's mother Rosie Lee was adamant that the child stay within the family and relayed her feelings in no uncertain terms to the facility's officials. A search was on for a home for the yet-to-be-born baby. Wanda's father (Curtis Lee Jones)'s sister, Ellen, and her husband, Fred Jarrell, a middle-aged childless couple, agreed to take the child.

Rosie Lee McClain Wilson (Wanda's Mother)

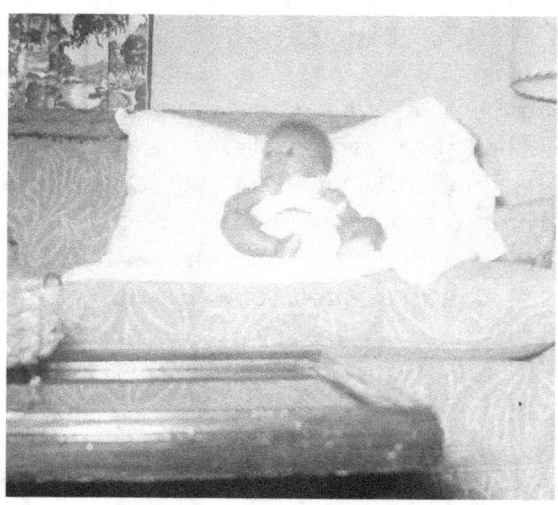

Baby Reggie Jarrell

Late one May Saturday night, Wanda delivered a healthy baby boy who she named Reginald Dean. She said she liked "Reginald" as it was the name of an actor. With a sparkle in her eye and a chuckle, years later Wanda recalled her first thought after seeing this baby she loved well before his birth: "You were ungodly ugly!"

The baby stayed with his mother's family until Ellen traveled alone on public transportation, to Kansas City to get him when he was three weeks old. Ellen admitted later to being quite anxious. She wanted to complete the trip as soon as possible after he was born.

"I was afraid Wanda was going to change her mind."
Like the bright expectation of the spring season, new mother Ellen returned to Wichita, Kansas with her son to start a new chapter in all of their lives. From that brief time with the Wilson family, the baby boy had his own brand-new family.

Rosie Lee and Wanda never provided any information to Ellen or Fred's side of the family about the biological father. Only a very few people on Rosie Lee's side of the family knew of the child's paternal identity. And these few select folks never shared what little information they had.

I was that baby. Little did I know it would take decades to discover who my biological father was. Eventually I wanted answers: Is he still alive? What is he like? Where is he? The bottom line, this was a journey to not only find my biological father, but myself.

In these pages Wanda is sometimes identified as "Nanny," her preferred moniker starting in the 1980's with the arrival of her grandchildren. "Mother" is always Ellen Jarrell unless otherwise noted and "Pop/Dad" refers to Fred Jarrell.

Beginnings
I have always known that Wanda was my real mother, meaning my biological mother. I can't remember any precise time or age that I was told by my adoptive parents, Fred and Ellen Jarrell who I called "Pop" and "Mother." It was always made clear that the young woman who was often around was Wanda McClain Grant. I remember being at my biological mother's wedding (at two or three I don't remember any details). How many other people, products of the 1950's cultures and traditions, can say that they were present at a parent's 1950's/early 60's era wedding as small children?

Knowing that Wanda was my "real" mother inevitably led to the question: "Who is my 'real' father?" And being too young to understand the complexities of adult relationships and sex, they would reply that my dad, Fred Jarrell, was my real father. That satisfied my childhood curiosity, at least for a while.

As a child, I admit, sometimes I would tell a few special and very close friends my secret, that I was adopted. I would share that my "real" mother lived in Kansas City and my dad who they knew as Mr. Jarrell was my "real" dad. Although I remember only one young friend actually questioning me more about that arrangement. Much later I would need further clarification. When that was I'm not exactly sure. Perhaps during those pre-teen years when I learned about the birds and the bees.

Thus, I did question the identity of my biological father when I got older. My eyes could see what could not be; Pop was a great deal older than Wanda. And besides, I could do the math. Fred Jarrell (actually my great uncle) was born in 1919, whereas Wanda, his niece, was born in 1943. Until then I had no reason to question what I'd been told. I began to understand why I was told Pop was my "real" dad. They knew if I was told Wanda was my "real" mother, I would ask other questions including the "real father" question. They knew I needed to have someone to identify as a "real" father instead of being told, "we don't know," which would lead other questions, for many of which they had no answers.

So, Wanda was always a part of my life. Usually it was "Frank and Wanda," Frank being her husband, and a wonderful man. Frank never treated me as a stepson, but as "son" and that was how he introduced me to his friends.

At four I remember jumping up and down on my bed with a wide, beaming grin, so excited at the news of the birth to Frank and Wanda of a girl, Tina. "I have a baby sister!" It was a scene of hysterical happiness and I remember Frank and Mother, Ellen Jarrell, also being in the room, witnesses to my joy.

Thus a part of my background was to me crystal clear: My family line included Wanda, her father, Curtis Lee Jones, aka Red Boy, Curtis's sister Ellen Jones Jarrell (Mother), and their parents, Thomas Bailey and Mary Liza Jones. As an adult I learned more about the great and greats, Thomas's father Calvin and his father Sam, who had been a slave in Texas by way of the Carolinas. Mary Liza's parents were George and Jane Long.

Many of these ancestors are buried in the small rural Black community cemetery of Huttonville, located just outside of Eufaula, Oklahoma.

Wanda's mother, Rose Wilson (Rosa/Rosie Lee) I was very familiar with, by way of family stories. Much later in life I learned the names of her parents.

But I knew nothing of the man who was my father. Throughout much of my young life, I really didn't care. I wasn't concerned with knowing. Then during my later teen years, at 16, 17 years, I started to wonder about the other side of my heritage. I started to face the truth that I didn't know anything about this side of me, whether I had another family. I began to ponder as my curiosity began to increase. Intensify.

This other side of me became, for many years a dark, heavily veiled mystery that I feared would never be solved. A mystery I wanted to solve before it was too late.

CHAPTER 1
First Steps

For years I had lingering questions about who I was, not from the standpoint of a lack of confidence or from insecurity, but from a longing to know more about my biological roots. Roots that for some reason Wanda just did not want to expose. As an adult I often longed for her to broach the subject, but she never did.

I remember once, before I got married, she wanted to talk with me. She was then married to Frank Grant and I had high hopes this was the moment I'd longed for.

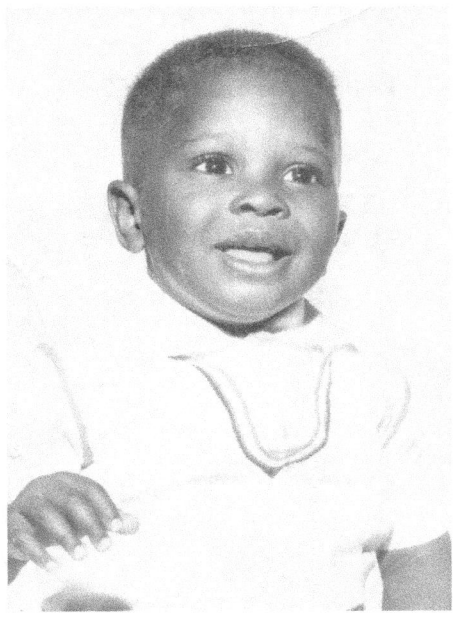

Reggie as baby

Mother and Pop Jarrell's home

Wanda McClain, 1958-59

Mother & Pop at our wedding

She was seated on a couch in the comfortable den of her Kansas City home with Frank. I grew anxious with keen anticipation. With Bible in hand, she discussed a particular scripture. Wanda provided none of the long awaited information about the man who was my biological father but gave an exposition on scripture and marriage, family, husband and wife as one. Man and woman clinging together.

No mention of my beginnings.

No conversation of who the mystery man was.

If I was going to get that information, I'd have to bring the subject up. I learned that for subjects she did not want to discuss she had a common response:

"The past is best left in the past."

Maybe I read into the statement more than she intended. Regardless, I took it that there were some topics she just didn't want to dig up out of the sands of time, some hurts she just didn't want to relive, some scabs she wouldn't scratch off. Still I longed to know. Fast forward several years, to the mid-1980's. My wife and I were living in New Orleans. Our sons Julian and Jonathan were born. Julian was born in Natchez, Mississippi while I was teaching at Alcorn State University and Jonathan was born in New Orleans while I was employed at Southern University in New Orleans. I had my own children now, Wanda was a grandmother we all called Nanny, and I still didn't know who my biological father was.

During a lull in a telephone conversation I decided then was as good a time as any to dive into *my* unknown past. So I asked. And I could tell by her reaction that the question caught her by surprise,

"What is my father's name?"

Nanny, the gracious, kind, caring, understanding and compassionate woman I'd always known as my "real" mother, didn't waver, or attempt to avoid the conversation. Instead of hijacking the conversation and taking it elsewhere, she answered. "Myron Clay."

It felt like the window shades of my life were beginning to rise.

I asked a few follow-up questions — what he looked like, how tall he was — but her answers were vague: "Oh, I can't really describe him, of average height."

But I had his name!

After all these years, a name.

I started doing research. This was long before the days of the internet and online ancestry databases. Using what are now old fashion techniques, skills I'd learned in journalism, with just his name, I found Myron's address in Kansas City.

This is more information than I'd ever had, but I had to weigh the pros and cons of carrying my search farther. I engaged in intense self-reflection as to the best next steps.

I decided to write Myron a letter of introduction. *How will he react? Will he respond?*

So many questions with unknown answers. I took nothing for granted, made no assumptions. Yet I had to launch into the deep, murky waters of the past to determine what, if anything, I could learn to help me understand who I was and from whence I came. All critical information, especially now that I had a family. *How would this new knowledge impact our future?*

So I wrote the letter. Short, succinct, to the point. From New Orleans where we were living. I mentioned who I was, referenced Wanda as my mother, and went from there.

After years of wondering and a rollercoaster ride of emotions, I mailed the letter.

The reply didn't take long.

Well, well! What do you know?!

About one week later, to my amazement, I received a response, and it was a positive response, from Myron Clay, Kansas City, Missouri. Myron acknowledged me. Reading between the lines he appeared just as pleased to receive my letter as I was when I finally learned his name. He invited me to call.

A phone call would put a voice behind that name. Yet a phone call was not as simple as it sounded. Easier said than actually done. To call meant inviting him into my world, becoming engaged with a man I knew nothing about. This would establish a link with him, between father and son, but I wasn't so sure I wanted to begin building this type of bridge. I was full of contradictions!

Isn't this what you wanted? Isn't this what this is about?
You can't open this door without stepping into his life!
Without him stepping into your life!
Did you just want to "know" but not get close?
Couldn't you see where this could lead?

I felt emotionally conflicted. Pop, Fred Jarrell was a great dad and still very much a part of my life. Myron was my biological father, but Pop was *Dad,* the only father I'd ever known. I embarked on an emotional rollercoaster ride. Ideas about the future, memories from the past, life in the present, all volleying for my consideration.

I remembered the story often told by Mother about our arrival in Wichita. It was late in the night and Mother had taken a taxi from the bus or train station. I was only a few weeks old. She brought me inside the small ranch style house they built on Piatt Avenue in 1951. Pop got up, stumbled from the bedroom, looked at me, and returned to bed without saying a word.

Mother put me to bed.

The next morning she got up, walked into the living room, and there Pop was, already up. but not alone. There this 5'8", 240 lb. sledge hammer of a strong man with biceps of a heavy weight lifter, sat in a chair, holding this small, dark-skinned baby in those huge arms. A man who gave a home to a child without one.

Any further dialogue with Myron would have to consider Pop.

My intense, personal, internal struggle was, Would it be fair to Pop? Would I be withdrawing from my relationship with Pop in establishing a relationship with Myron?

Questions. Conflict. Tension. Is this what I want? Do I need this? Now? Ever?

With mixed emotions I decided to do nothing, send no return letter, make no phone call, nothing. It was as if I left Myron hanging, after all those years.

When I told Wanda about my contact with Myron, she was both reserved and cautious. While not discouraging any additional contact and leaving it up to me, she passed on her mother Rosie Lee's warning to stay away from him.

"My mother told me never to have anything to do with that man," Wanda said. "But she never said why." I wanted to read into that statement but ultimately still it was just speculation.

Was her mother's comment the reason she was not forthcoming with information?

What did Rosie Lee sense, or know, that prompted this warning?

Was Myron really that bad?

I took to heart both Wanda's warning and Rosie Lee's message from the grave. There would be no communication, no contact, no nothing with Myron Clay. Zilch. For decades.

Her warning and the truth would take on a different meaning many years later, once I learned more about Myron.

At this time I was in my mid- to late 20's, with a lot more of life to learn.

CHAPTER 2
Nanny/Wanda

"How are you doing Mr. Jarrell?"

For years, after my children were born, that was Wanda's greeting. Before that, when I was a child, she called me by the family nickname, "Skeeter." However, when I grew up and became a young man, it was usually "Reggie" and sometimes, when opening a phone call, "Mr. Jarrell." Intermingled among those monikers was the loving term of endearment, "Son."

Small in stature, olive and cream complexioned, Nanny was a wise, no nonsense, take care of business, independent minded, discerning, freethinking sparkplug before the women's liberation movement. About 5-foot-4 inches tall, her back and shoulders erect, her walk sure and her step confident, Nanny also had a way of knowing just the right time to speak. Her speech was measured and thoughtful, as in the adage "less is more."

And as there were only fourteen years between us, I witnessed her maturation. I remember visiting her when she was a young wife in the small brick home in Northeast Wichita, just a short walk from Wichita State University. She and husband Frank later moved to Kansas City, Missouri. I remember my first and only train ride to Kansas City for a summer visit, tapping up the stairs of an old two-story house they rented. During this visit I called her "mother" but it didn't quite feel right and didn't last long. Mother was at home in Wichita, Kansas. My young mind couldn't really comprehend calling two women "mother" and I returned to calling her what I'd always called her, "Wanda."

Wanda's Father "Red Boy" Curtis Lee Jones

Wanda, 13, with Red Boy's other children, Christmas, 1956

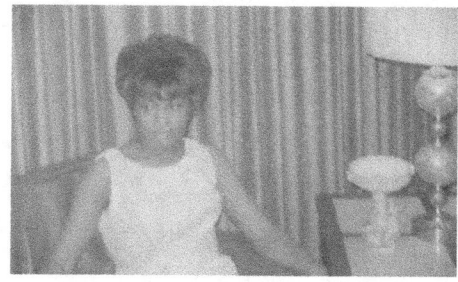

Wanda McCain Grant at her home in Kansas City

As a child I saw Wanda, then twenty-something, as street wise, but a hip, cool, cigarette smoking, "relative" who showed me how to dance and always treated me kindly. She could really maneuver the sparkling, fire red two-door 1960's stick shift Chevy, speeding up and down Kansas City's hilly streets, punching the gears with the best of them.

Years later, when I was a teen, she was a mature, insightful, unselfish, knowledgeable, wise, considerate, Christian adult. It was after a church service celebrating the graduating seniors that Wanda, caught in a gentle moment of introspection, shed tears.

"I'm proud of you," she said.

She had said that often; she was never short on praise or compliments. But this time she added, "I was a child, trying to raise a child."

Wanda was forever appreciative to Mother and Pop for taking me. She clearly understood her early teen limitations.

I cannot remember a time that Wanda was not a part of my life. And I was always thrilled when she would come to town, she made me feel special. For special occasions there were always wonderful gifts, but I always enjoyed being around her as I felt her genuine concern.

For several years, during the summer Wanda and Frank would take a vacation with Frank's sister Anne and her husband Bob and would bring the children: my sister Tina, Anne and Bob's daughter Marsha, me and, sometime another cousin or two. We would travel by car to some exciting destination. One time it was Six Flags over Texas. Another it was beautiful Colorado Springs. One Colorado trip provided a lasting memory of Wanda's personality.

We had been driving around town and were looking for something to eat.

"Do you like pizza?" Wanda quizzed.

"No, I don't like pizza," came my nine-year-old reply.

Wanda, insightful as ever, took it another step."Have you ever had pizza?"

"No, but I know I don't like it. I like hamburgers"

"How do you know you won't like it?"

"I just know."

Wanda didn't miss a beat. She didn't brow beat me, didn't make any snide or hurtful comments, didn't humiliate her son. She understood me.

That evening while everyone else munched on pizza I enjoyed my hamburger.

Many summers I'd spend a week or so in Kansas City, and I have many memories of the first house Wanda and Frank purchased, a small split-level ranch on Indiana Street. After the birth of my sister Erika — Wanda and Frank's youngest child who was born ten years after Tina — in the mid-1970's the family moved to much larger, traditional two-story Tudor-style home in an established integrated neighborhood not far from highway I-435. Wherever Wanda lived, she kept the house clean and tidy, every item in its place, with décor reminiscent of *Better Homes and Gardens.* She also worked full time for several businesses including AT&T, Sunshine Foods, Gamin Technology International, and later in life she worked as a certified nurse's assistant and operator/ owner of her own home health care business, Wanda's Agape Care.

I was comfortable visiting Kansas City, there was always a bedroom for me, but it wasn't *my* home. Sometimes when I visited, as a child, I would get seriously homesick. I could not wait to get back home to Wichita even though I was around folks who sincerely loved me. A few times my week or two visit had to be cut short because of my homesickness.

Wanda never complained or made me feel guilty. No deep, agonizing sighs, no rolling of the eyes, fits of exasperation, nothing. I never felt any negativity whatsoever from her regarding how I may have felt. It was as if she *understood.*

When I grew older, I learned her story. She was an illegitimate baby herself, born in Indianapolis, living with her mother Rosie Lee in Kansas City, but also spending time with her father Curtis, grandparents, and other relatives in Oklahoma. Perhaps she felt like a bouncing ball going place to place, sometimes landing in not the happiest situations. Wanda understood the importance of acceptance and love. She understood what that meant to a child struggling to find a place not only in the world, but also within their own family.

I mentioned that Wanda's father, Curtis Lee Jones, was affectionately known as Red Boy because of his complexion. Mother and other family members always spoke highly, even reverently about the kindness of this big, gentle, compassionate, personable man. When she was born her father was seventeen and her mother fifteen, and she spent time among both extended families, Rosie's Lee's parents, Charles McClain and Willie Gilkey Johnston, and Red Boy's mother, Mary Liza Jones.

Wanda experienced heartbreak and pain early in life. Before she was a teenager, a seemingly innocent, festive holiday drive turned into tragedy. Red Boy was killed in a highway traffic accident on Mother's Day, 1955. He'd been driving in the early morning dark to Huttonville, Oklahoma to see his mother. Red Boy was always known as a "fast driver." Red Boy was apparently sideswiped by a truck just a few miles outside of Kansas City. It was said he was killed instantly. Wanda was twelve.

Wanda's mother Rosie Lee would also be taken before the prime of her life. She would often get headaches and after one episode, apparently she fainted. She was rushed to a hospital and told she needed an operation. But Rosie Lee had a premonition which she shared with Wanda.

"If they go inside my head," she warned, lying in the hospital bed, "I won't make it."

It was not her husband Bernard but Wanda who Rosie Lee wanted to see to the difficult business decisions regarding her death. She spoke of her insurance policy and how to take care of arrangements, apparently knowing Wanda could and would properly handle business issues. When Rosie Lee finished talking to her daughter, she turned her back and would not look at her again. It was an agonizing, heartbreaking goodbye.

Rosie Lee had the brain operation, and as she predicted, things did not go well. She survived the surgery but lapsed into a coma for several days and never awakened. Rosie Lee slept into eternity.

Wanda was at home when Bernard returned from the hospital. "Your momma died," he announced.

Wanda was eighteen.

Hard times, difficult situations but everything was not dark. There was the tall, handsome, and kind Frank Grant. They met while both were students at Wichita East High School. Frank was two grades ahead of Wanda. Clearly he was a special man to fall in love with and fully accept a woman with a small child she had given for adoption. A child who was still part of her family and with whom she continued to be involved.

It never mattered to Frank. I will always be thankful for the man he was and his total acceptance of me. He was a wonderful man. They stayed together for decades, and their divorce, in the mid 1980's, surprised many family members. All Wanda would say, several years later, was that they would have stayed together if not for Frank's mother. She did not elaborate and I never posed any follow up questions.

Although I was quite young, I attended Frank and Wanda's wedding. I don't remember details but I remember the festive, happy occasion. The venue was an African Methodist Episcopal Church which later housed a Church of God In Christ congregation. The church is just two blocks away from my childhood home on Piatt Avenue. If memory serves me correctly, the only other time I was in that edifice was more than forty years later, January 2006, for Mother's (Ellen's) homegoing celebration.

Pure joy, Wanda's bouncy, lighthearted laughter was the hallmark of her personality. Over the years our relationship became more than mother-son, and more a close-knit friendship. I grew to confide in and trust her opinion, and, while she wasn't one to often tell me what to do, she'd offer insight and an objective view of the situation. And she always seemed to know just what to do say, when to say it, and how to say it. Even if she uttered few words.

Many years later, married and with three children, we were living in a duplex in Davenport, Iowa and I faced an incident that could have, but for the grace of God, turned into a tragic, life changing moment.

We had a small dog, Diamond, a black and white terrier, and I was walking her across the street from our duplex. A middle aged, Caucasian, boyfriend of the resident of the next door duplex, drove by in his truck, stopped, and exited from his truck. What he said lit a match of anger within me. "I wish I had a n------ to walk."

I was shocked. We'd never had any trouble whatsoever from anyone, and this was completely out of the blue.

"What did you say?"

Keeping his back turned, still heading for the door of his girlfriend's duplex, he repeated his offensive comment.

My first thought was to let it go, ignore his ignorance, let it be. This foolish man doesn't know me. But my second thought took control. Another voice, an angry voice. "This ain't the 1950's" played over and over in my mind. "You don't have to take that!" And what started as an innocent walk with a tiny dog boiled over into a simmering rage ready to explode in violence.

I went back to our duplex, let the dog go, and went looking for Old Betsy.

Let's see how he talks to Old Betsy.

Old Betsy was the nickname of my barely legal, short barrel 12-gauge shotgun that for many years I traveled within the trunk of my car.

I grabbed Old Betsy but there was a problem, a big problem.

The shotgun was unloaded and in those moments of anger, I could not remember where I put my shells. I'm walking through the duplex, gun in hand, telling my wife Canetha what had just happened but not thinking clearly enough to remember where my shells were. I was very aware of an essential lesson learned from Pop: never show a gun unless it's loaded. The other person doesn't know it's unloaded and if he has a gun...

I knew I couldn't walk out with an unloaded gun, but it wasn't over. So I walked out of my duplex, onto to the sidewalk facing the front of the duplex to confront the visiting racist. He wasn't coming out, he wasn't opening the door, he wasn't parting the drapes, he wasn't doing anything. I returned to my duplex. Then back outside again. I repeated this several times to no avail. He wouldn't come out.

I called the police and, after getting the royal run around, was told, "We don't handle neighborhood disputes like that." I told the dispatcher, "You've been warned, and you've been told. If something happens and someone gets hurt, don't say you weren't called. I called for help and you did nothing."

The dispatcher's tune immediately changed. She would send someone out, immediately. I was still boiling, straining, trying to recall where my shells were, but I still could not remember. Canetha later admitted she knew but wasn't about to tell me. At the time I was close friends with a deacon from our church. So I called and asked if he could come over.

This great friend, William Baugh, came and stayed. For hours. The police came as well. Found out the racist was well known to the police. The racist would not answer the door; he obviously knew the police were there. While they didn't make an arrest, they gave me an update. After several hours, my mind settled, thanks to the peaceful insight of Canetha and the calming reassurance of my dear friend.

After I had cooled and thought things through clearly, I understood the ramifications of what could have been. And the potential headlines:

"Rock Island Attorney Arrested for Attempted Murder"
"Local Church Official Shoots and Kills Visiting Neighbor"
"Shootout at Davenport Duplex"

It could have been real ugly. I could have lost everything with my life destroyed because I slipped into evil's trap.

The next day I apologized to my church family (but another preacher tagged me with the label "Rev. Shotgun"). I wondered what I would do when I saw the offender again. I never did. I never saw him return to the duplex.

I rarely shared racial incidents, even major ones, with others. No need to relive painful experiences by repeating the stories, yet I had to tell Wanda about this one particularly painful experience. She should know about this time.

I thought I knew how she would react. I expected her to say, "That's right, you stand up for yourself, You take care of business, those days are over! Stand up to any bully, any time!" or something along those lines.

Her response was nothing like that. Two words is all I remember, that and her tone. A mournful sigh, "Oh, Reggie." And that said it all. She knew as I did the anger I had felt. She understood fully as she understood who and what I was. But that was all that she needed to say.

Wanda was always caring and compassionate, always clear and direct when it came to professing and showing her love. But, of course, we had our disagreements. Two of them were related to young women that I dated. The first was Margaret, a relationship I had when I was a senior in high school. She was Caucasian and Wanda was concerned about our safety.

"Be careful" she cautioned, "everyone is not thoughtful or kind."

The other young woman, African American, I'll call Diane, I dated in college and Wanda just didn't care for her personality. Diane was the smart, sophisticated, an "open and close the door for me" kind of lady who enjoyed the finer things in life. She could also be argumentative and stubborn. While Wanda appreciated Diane's intelligence and sense of style, Wanda was old school in her view that women should be independent, open their own doors, make their way in the world while taking care of business.

Yet when she was around both young ladies, Wanda always treated them with kindness and respect. It was only after both relationships had ended that I learned the full extent of her feelings.

Wanda did not say or do anything disparaging or derogatory regarding the young women. Neither did she ever interfere in any way. Wanda clearly understood about being involved with someone from "across the tracks" who the family might not accept, or a partner who is difficult, stubborn, and increases stress. Relationships, like life, impact health and Wanda had her share of serious health challenges.

In 1996, Wanda was returning from her first Caribbean cruise. She had a wonderful time with other relatives and friends. The vacation was over, and the travelers were returning home. They had arrived in the United States and had made it to their hotel in Dallas when things changed. Wanda mentioned a headache; she wasn't feeling well. Then she fainted in the lobby.

Aunt Ruth Jones, Mother's youngest sister, told of a mysterious older man who was among the spectators. From his description, it seemed that this gentleman looked a bit out of place. In the chaos, there were plenty of onlookers, but no one was taking any action. Suddenly this rumpled, unassuming stranger knelt down and administered CPR to Wanda until the emergency medics arrived. One of the emergency personnel indicated that someone had administered excellent CPR, but when Aunt Ruth looked to acknowledge the gentleman, he was nowhere to be found. Gone. Just like that he had vanished. He didn't stick around to see what the outcome would be, as if he knew she would be all right.

In extremely critical condition Wanda was taken to one local hospital, then transferred to another, this one being a facility that specialized in brain injuries. Some hospital personnel indicated her condition was grave and she might not survive.

But she did and surgery was scheduled for a few days later, once her condition stabilized. Wanda was in the best possible place; brain surgery and aneurysms were what they dealt with routinely.

We were cautioned that she might not survive the procedure. But Wanda wasn't worried. In the midst of the biggest crisis, the most dangerous storm she had faced in life, she was at peace. "It's going to be okay," she whispered to me. There was no fear, no worry in her eyes. Going through a life-threatening situation similar to what had taken her mother decades ago, Wanda was a picture of calm, a solid pillar of faith, strength, and power.

She went through the procedure well and spent several weeks recovering. After rehabilitation she bounced back, but she retained no memory of the Dallas events and the agonizing time in that Dallas hospital. As if it hadn't happened. Wanda was herself again. "Nanny" was back.

Wanda at son Jonathan's H.S. grad with Regina

Fast forward about ten years to the spring of 2007. Life began to shift for Wanda. She suffered her first stroke, which affected some of her physical capabilities, but after therapy once again she bounced back to life as usual and returned to routine activities such as teaching Sunday School, walking around the block, gardening, handling household chores, driving, and running errands. She had retired and was enjoying, as she said, "doing absolutely nothing" she didn't want to do.

But on December 24, 2008, Wanda's world crashed. It was another stroke, but this one affected her mentally and physically. After several months, there followed yet another stroke and seizures. She was in and out of hospitals, medical facilities, and home. Her condition was up and down, her logic and rational thinking abilities impaired. She mixed reality with fantasy, the past with the present. She even, at times, was confused about who I was, dividing her only son into separate and very different persons.

Although Wanda returned home and was back to doing her usual routine tasks, clearly her mental state was inconsistent. Once, my sister Erika had stopped by and we were chatting in the den when Wanda entered the room and joined our conversation.

"Skeeter came in last night," Wanda said to us, clearly referring to someone not in the room and certainly not to me, although I was standing just a few steps away, directly facing her.

"There's Skeeter right here," Erika pointed out to Wanda.

"Oh yeah, that's right, I forgot." Wanda covered her confusing Reginald or Reggie (the adult) with Skeeter. (the child). At times I was not sure who she thought I was. Sometimes I could see in her eyes and behavior that she viewed me as a stranger.

Seizures and strokes continued. More hospitalizations. Finally, in the spring of 2010, surgery was done to stop bleeding in her brain and repair additional aneurysms. The brain hemorrhage was stopped but the consequences tragic.

Wanda was left paralyzed. She could turn her head, but only slightly move an arm. She was totally, completely bedridden. The feisty, independent, strong, take-care-of-business woman was gone. Forever. Many years Wanda had been a healthcare worker providing for others. Now she was the one who needed to be cared for. During many earlier conversations we had talked about people she cared for, people in dreadful conditions who could do little or nothing for themselves.

"They have life, but there's no quality of life," she'd say. "They are just existing." Still she sought to bring love, joy, comfort and peace to those patients in discomfort. Wanda was a bridge of hope to many in difficult situations. Now Wanda was experiencing what her patients experienced, she was bound to that life. She was a shell of herself.

Wanda stopped talking. She could go for weeks or longer without uttering a single word. But her eyes told her story. The spark extinguished, the gleam dulled. Sadness. Despair. Pain. In Wanda's eyes.

Lord have mercy!

I missed Wanda, Nanny, my mother, my friend.

How I longed to see her smile, hear her laughter once again.

Our ways are not God's ways, our thoughts are not God's thoughts. I don't know why but that was between God and Wanda. Yet my prayer continued to thank God for her and to ask for grace and mercy, comfort and peace.

Wanda had been a longtime, active church worker at Mt. Vernon Missionary Baptist Church, performing various roles — Sunday School teacher, usher ministry, editor of the church history book. She was also a gifted public speaker and relished the opportunity to witness to others. Most importantly, she believed in God, lived her faith accordingly, and practiced the mandate: "treat all people right."

Wanda lingered in her bedridden state for six years. She did not speak a single sentence to me after her surgery, but she listened, and oh did she listen. It was the clear, laser beam like focus of her eyes that told you she engaged in your conversation.

During this challenging time, although I understood this was between God and Wanda. I often lamented: *Lord, how long?*

CHAPTER 3
Fathers

Growing up, there were plenty of men who served as examples of a father, both outside and inside my family. They included several uncles, Uncles Penney, Ruester, Floyd, Pete, Lucious and O.T., who all made indelible contributions to my personality and character. Each provided invaluable lessons on family, God, love, and being a man. But there were other models as well: one was that of the hardnosed, strong, never-shed-a-tear patriarch.

Within in my circle of friends I knew few single parent households headed by women. Yet despite the presence of dads in some families, to be quite honest, I was glad I was not part of some of those households.

I saw firsthand the stern, harsh, take-no-prisoners, cut-no-slack, "I'm a MAN and it is going to be my way or I have something to convince and persuade you of my authority" father of some friends. Friends who appeared, at times, scared to death of their fathers. Perhaps that's what some boys needed, a firm hand, but, even as a child, I often questioned if that really was the most productive way to rear children, especially sons. Fathers who were feared just didn't seem to me what a father ought to be.

Thank God, Pop was nothing like that. Physically strong, certainly. Anyone who worked hard labor at the flour milling company, loading heavy flour sacks onto trucks and railroad cars 365 days a year in below freezing ice, sleet, and snow as well as 100 degree-plus heat for more than 25 years had to be strong. He had a tank-like chest with power hammer arms.

But Pop was a quiet, unassuming, hardworking man who was indeed always there for me. He was not perfect and made his share of mistakes, some of which I readily picked up on as a teenager, but he was a loving and caring father who always sought my best interests. To be clear, I loved and accepted Pop as my father from day one. He was the only father that I knew. He never gave me a reason *not* to like him.

Pop didn't graduate from high school and while I'm not sure how far he got, he may not have finished junior high school. Regardless, he could handle money; he not only understood the value of a dollar but he was second to none when it came to saving and budgeting. He believed in hard work but also understood the importance of paying yourself first and saving for a rainy day. Pop also understood how to make money work for the family, the importance of insurance and certificates of deposit and bonds. It was well known within his community of family and friends that Fred Jarrell had more than just a few pennies stashed away in the bank. It was also not unusual for Pop to carry several thousand dollars in his wallet. When he bought new cars, he paid cash.

"Somebody's going to knock you in the head and take your money," Mother would sometimes warn.

Somebody hitting and robbing him was the least of Pop's concerns. Only a fool would think of trying such a thing. And if someone did try, that man would be wise to turn himself in to the police for the safety of the county jail. Pop boxed as a young man, and Mother often told the story of how he whipped two three-hundred-pound brothers at one time.

Pop worked hard labor for more than thirty years, as a miller/packer at the Kansas Milling Company and later Cargill Industries. At retirement he was only credited for just over twenty-five years, although he actually worked there longer. He told me he worked for ten to fifteen years and then quit, and after working someplace else in Wichita, they asked him to return to the mill because of his attitude and work ethic. He did so, but the bureaucrats did not give him credit for all those prior years; he did not take a cut in pay, and he was more than satisfied with what his wages were so didn't care about not being given credit for his earlier years on the job. Pop knew exactly what was going on, so it was not a matter of being taken advantage of by the company's administrators. I still believe that decision was unfair and he was cheated. But Pop was not bitter or angry about it. He made the best out of the situation for probably one reason: he loved to work. Perhaps he loved feeling productive and satisfied with his lot in life. Pop put 110 percent effort into his job, every hour, every day.

Many times Pop would come home after working an exhausting eight hour or longer shift and go to bed only to receive a call asking him to return to work for another shift. "Is Fred there?" came the voice on the phone.

Sometimes I wanted to say, "Yes, but he's sleeping/resting/had enough for the day." But I didn't. And I knew what Pop would do. Pop would answer the phone, respond in the affirmative, get dressed, and return to work. Regardless of weather. Regardless of how he felt. Regardless of what other things might have been going on in the family.

"Fred is going to die at the mill," family members used to joke.

Work was his passion and his outlet.

There were few family vacations; in fact, the number of times all three of us traveled together out of town could be counted on one hand. Most of the time it was Mother and me. If Pop took time off from work, which was rare, he'd just stick around the house in his ever present blue bib overalls (having changed out of the white flour and dust covered overalls from work).

Pop didn't die at the mill, but the years of hard labor without adequate rest and physical recovery certainly took their toll on his body. The hard labor that, as I used to joke, resulted in his arms being the size of my legs, produced a strength building program that would rival any structured program at a local gym. During his later years his body, ravished by those hard years of labor, broke down. His chest showed a patchwork pattern of scars from enduring several major surgeries, including several heart surgeries. Due to heart disease and diabetes Pop dropped a great deal of weight. He lost some hearing from the mill's loud clanging conveyor belts. But he never complained. He never went the woulda-shoulda-coulda route about anything, including his health. The only exception was when he stopped work early due to that first health issue (heart problems) and realized what he had been missing. He started to relish taking life slow and easy. He did not *miss* getting up and going to work every day.

Pop worked hard but I have so many, many other memories that provide comfort in the decades after his death. As a small child Saturday morning we made trips to the bakery for a dozen glazed donuts, most of which I would eat during the ride home. Mother would often cook an egg and bacon breakfast on Saturdays, and I'd continue eating donuts when we got home. Pop never complained about this, although he rarely got a donut. I can still taste those heavily glazed bastions of sweet pleasure to this day.

I remember Pop picking me up from Ingalls Elementary School, four to five blocks from home. I usually walked both to and from school, but sometimes for lunch he would take me to a hamburger haven housed in a small, white-painted building on the corner of 17th Street and Mosley. I can still smell the aroma of grilled burgers wafting through the door. To this day I measure burgers against those from my childhood. Pop would order my favorites: hamburger with mustard and pickle, and a package of Hostess chocolate, vanilla-filled cupcakes. Never any fries or drink.

During those elementary school days there was always a field day in the spring near the end of school. It was an all-school track and field meet where the classes from each grade competed against each other. Pop could always be counted on to be there for my races regardless of the time he had to work.

Oh, how I looked forward to seeing him in those in those ever present blue bib overalls topped off with his flour covered cap. I would scan the crowd of parents standing and cheering — there were no bleachers — and Pop never disappointed; he was always there.

Pop was a staunch believer in education, although he dropped out of school at an early age to help on the family farm in Oklahoma.

"If you want to go to college, I'll help you," he would say. He never tried to push me in any particular direction or to any specific employment. It was always clear that I had his support whatever direction I wanted to go.

Often Pop would sit at the dining room table and flip the pages of the daily newspaper. Notice I said "flip the pages," looking at the photographs and the ads. I never saw him read an article or pick up a magazine or book, and I'm not sure how well he could read. When I was in high school or college, sometimes when he received business letters, he would have me read them and then tell him what the letter said.

Pop was a quiet man with a wide grin, and one top, front tooth bordered in gold, part of a bridge. Pop's Native American and Caucasian heritage were apparent in his jet black straight hair, broad face, and a light complexion. He could have "passed" for Caucasian: I believe his oldest sister, Lilly, did just that. All of his sisters were fair-skinned with long straight hair and could have "passed."

Lilly left the Oklahoma family farm as a young woman and moved to New York City never to return. Only one of her sisters maintained contact with her, but even that stopped after a few years.

Pop's father, Robert, was a farmer in the predominantly Black town of Rentiesville, Oklahoma, while his mother, Dora, tended to the family of six children. Pop's father hailed from Georgia and did not know who his father was. The story told by family members was that Pop's father Robert was "raised" by a Caucasian man in Georgia on a farm or plantation. The man treated him very well to the consternation of other Caucasians in that community. When Robert's life and family were threatened, this man put them on a train, giving them $10,000 to start life over in Oklahoma. Robert was a dark-skinned man with straight hair and Caucasian facial features. His mother Dora was of Native American descent.

I can't remember a single instance where Pop ever raised his voice. He could get excited watching professional wrestling, but he did not yell like other dads. Nor was he harsh, stern, hard hearted, or mean spirited. He had a wide, gleaming smile and a joyful, hearty laugh that I miss to this day.

In my search for my biological father I realized that no one could ever compete with or replace Pop. In his life he never made a distinction or commented in a derogatory way about me not being his biological or "natural" son; it never came up and he never, ever gave me any indication that such a thought ever crossed his mind. I was his son plain and simple. That's the way it was and would always be.

Pop was a man who kept his promises. I've mentioned that when Mother first brought me home to Wichita from Kansas City, she had awakened the very next morning to find Pop holding me in his arms. She recounted the story frequently of Pop declaring to my tiny self that: "When you grow up I'm going to buy you a brand new car!"

Many years later, before I was "legal" to drive, before my sixteenth birthday, he made good on his promise.

One Sunday afternoon Pop took me to an Oldsmobile dealership and we walked the new car lot. The dealership was closed, so there were no constantly smiling, firm handshaking salespersons with hopes for a commission there. We walked the lot surrounded by a plethora of sparkling, gleaming Cutlass models, a popular model at that time.

"Pick one," Pop said.

Although I was well aware of his long ago promise, still I was shocked. I just didn't expect it to be filled then and there.

And I couldn't pick one. I just felt the Olds Cutlass, although very nice, just wasn't my kind of car. The brand new cars on this lot just were not the right fit for me, although Pop's work car that I'd been tooling around town in was, in fact, a 1965 blue, two-door with console in the floor, an Olds Cutlass.

A few weeks later I was returning home from school one day, again driving Pop's car. As I approached our house, I saw a two-tone, gold with white trim car sitting in the drive.

What's going on? I wondered.

Mother and Pop met me outside, before I could enter the house.

"What's happening?" I asked, or something to that effect.

"It's your car."

Shocked, I remember breaking into a wide smile, shaking Pop's hand, and opening the door to *my car* with its new car smell.

It was a 1973 Ford Maverick Grabber with tan bucket seats, white vinyl top, and a flashy gold with white trim paint job. I took the car for a drive, stopping by a few friends and relatives.

That was March, 1973, two months before my 16th birthday.

Pop had made good on his promise.

The stories could go on. When my sons were born, Pop was indeed the loving Grandpa. Son Jonathan was barely six months old when we spent the summer in Wichita. I was in transition, having left my teaching job in New Orleans and to start law school in the fall of 1984. Pop spent many days walking with Julian, who wasn't yet two years old. They'd walk on the sidewalk or Pop would trail Julian as he rode his toddler trike. Sometimes he'd sit in his rocking chair, under a tree in the front yard, rocking Jonathan.

It was the end of the fall semester of my second year in law school, at the beginning of our December finals when I got word that Pop had suffered another heart attack. I had last chatted with him on Thanksgiving. His voice had been a bit weak, but he said he had been feeling fine. He was looking forward to Christmas. This latest heart attack caught me by surprise. He had been outside scraping ice off Mother's car. He came inside the house and collapsed on the dining room floor. Emergency personnel were called, and Pop made it to the hospital, but he had suffered some brain damage.

Pop holding Julian

Pop and dog

I flew to Wichita where Pop was in a coma for a few days before he regained consciousness. The weight he had lost watching his diet and walking several blocks a day, taking good care of himself, was obvious. There he was, my once strong, muscle-bound Pops, conscious, paralyzed, and unable to speak.

That holiday season was a blur as we traveled back and forth to the hospital, hoping, praying for a full recovery. Visualizing Pop being Pop again, healed and restored.

They transferred Pop to another local hospital, and I felt I could return to school. There was talk about rehab for Pop, and I thought, in time, he would be okay. It was New Year's Day, and Mother and I were visiting Pop. His eyes were wide open, and he was listening. I wasn't going to tell him I was leaving town to return to school — I was just going to keep it simple and say goodbye. But Mother urged me to tell him. I never will forget that as I started telling him I was leaving to return to law school, Pop, who had been attentive and alert the entire visit, closed his eyes and did not open them again. I told him that I would be back and see him again at spring break or sometime. I started to kiss him on his forehead, something I'd never done before, but I decided against it. That would be out of character. Besides, I was confident that we would talk again.

The following Sunday morning in Iowa City, I went to a grocery to pick up a newspaper. When I returned to our apartment, Canetha gave me the news: Pop had died.

I could not believe it. He was doing so well. He was going to make it, a full recovery. It was not to be. I realized the significance of his closing his eyes. He knew. January 5, 1986, he was gone. A stranger who became my daddy, Dad, Pop, and my friend, my advisor, my role model. The man who provided not only stability but comfort. The man who offered unconditional love to a tiny baby who needed a family.

The man who was my father.

Pop was 66 years old.

CHAPTER 4
Mother (Ellen Jarrell)

When I think of my family I generally think of my family on my adoptive mother's side. Mother, Ellen Jones Jarrell, was the older sister of Curtis Lee Jones, aka "Red Boy," my birthmother Wanda's father.

Like Pop, Mother was born in 1919. She was the third oldest of eleven children, and she grew up on a farm near Huttonville, Oklahoma, just outside of Eufaula. Her dad, Thomas Bailey Jones, was a farmer who had served in the U.S. Army in World War I. Life was tough on the farm, but Tom and Mother's mother Mary Liza did what they could to survive. Both Tom and Mary Liza had migrated from Texas to Oklahoma on wagon trains with their families.

Mother graduated from an all-Black high school in Huttonville in 1940 and married Pop two years later in Kansas City, Missouri. She had some health issues and could not have children. By the time I was born, Pop and Mother were in their late thirties.

As Mother recounted the story, when Wanda was pregnant, her mother, Rosie Lee, was looking to keep me within the family. Another sister, Cleo, was approached about raising me, but she could not due to her job. That was a blessing. Although Wanda never said so, the family knew that Cleo sometimes exhibited a dominating, controlling, cruel, and manipulative personality. It would not have been a pleasant environment for me to grow up in. Wanda lived a year or so in Cleo's household after I was born while she was in high school and indicated that living in Cleo's household was stressful.

Fortunately, another couple, also relatives, did have room in their household. Ellen and Fred Jarrell opened their doors and agreed to raise me as their own.

Mother (Ellen) was wise, compassionate, understanding, patient, encouraging, and loving. I usually got my choice of clothing, toys, activities. I could count on my favorite cake, chocolate, for birthdays. And Pop was a solid provider for his family.

There are distinct advantages to growing up as an only child: there was no competition for attention. Mother taught many essential lessons for success in life, including to always do my very best regardless of the circumstances. Mother also emphasized the importance of studying as well as reading. She introduced me to those wonderful Little Golden Books of children's stories. She encouraged my public speaking skills for church Christmas and Easter children's programs — I performed speeches, plays, and songs.

All folk have their personality quirks, and Mother could be judgmental and critical. And sometimes Mother said and did some things that she just should not have said or done. I believe that she always had my best interests at heart, and that she indeed loved me from day one, but her idiosyncrasies could hurt. After I grew up, sometimes we simply did not see eye to eye.

After Pop died in 1986, Mother changed, for the better. During the twenty years that she lived after Pop's death, Mother learned to say, "I am sorry" and regretted some of the things she had previously said or done. Mother became more open minded, flexible, understanding, generous, and sharing. She grew in wisdom and compassion. Mother was living proof that people can change for the better.

Before I was born Mother worked at a local aircraft plant. After I was born, she stopped working until my teen years when she worked part-time as a domestic for some Caucasian families.

She enjoyed getting out of the house, although I did not like her working as a domestic. They had a solid bank account, so she did not *have to* work. But I learned to accept her decision because it was something she wanted to do. She only worked for a handful of families over the years and became quite close to a couple of the families. I met members of one of the families and they were sincerely nice people. Mother often said that she wanted to do the best she could in anything that she attempted, and that was true. She emphasized that one should do one's best, regardless.

She was a masterful gardener, with a green thumb that she demonstrated by a garden in the back yard and an array of beautiful flowers on the front, back, and sides of the house. Mother brought in as many flowering plants as she could to save them from the harsh, bitter cold during the winter, and they graced the house, primarily in our den.

Mother became active in a small, Baptist church when I was young, serving as a Sunday School teacher and being involved with other ministries for many years. She faithfully served Jesus Christ, God, and believed in the power of prayer, both personal and corporate. Mother was a strong, believing, praying woman, a "prayer warrior" who would enlist fellow church prayer warriors to pray for God's help, sometimes on my behalf. I appreciated her concern as well as her seeking others to pray for me. She modeled dedication in reading Scripture.

For years her bedtime routine included sitting on the edge of her bed, glasses hugging her nose, reading that week's Sunday School lesson or her Bible.

In my quest to find my father, I started to ask questions. Mother simply did not know any of the answers. Yet she was never defensive. She never gave the impression that she was offended nor threatened. Mother seemed to understand my curiosity. After I had children, Mother and I used to have some fascinating discussions around the dining room table, covering a plethora of subjects from current events, politics, racism, religion, church, and current events to children and family. There were always magazines and newspapers in the house and Mother was well informed. I never tired of chatting with her.

For years, wherever we lived, Mother would call once a week just to check in. And usually wherever we lived Mother would come for a visit unless she or Pop had health issues.

Yet Mother knew she would not live forever and the best time to prepare was well before disease and illness started taking their toll on her mind and body.

Mother taught me how to die gracefully. When she started having health issues — kidney issues which required dialysis in the mid-1990's, cancer, or something else — she kept me informed but always understood my family responsibilities. I would come to Wichita as often as I could while we were living in Davenport, Iowa, to do what I could for her. Sometimes that just meant being present. Although she had been hospitalized from time to time or one ailment or another, she was still quite active. Mother had stopped driving but was still attending church, running errands, living her normal life.

In the early 2000's, after another health flareup, I came home for a visit, and Mother forecast her last days would be challenging.

After her cancer diagnosis, Mother slowly ambled around the house, dressed in her housecoat as we chatted about her health. Her face was relaxed, her gaze peaceful. Then Mother let me know that she was ready, and I needed to be ready.

"I am going to get worse, much worse."

No, no, no. My initial thoughts of disbelief.

But Mother was going to face her biggest health challenge with faith and courage, as she did life. As her health began to deteriorate in 2004, sometimes she would bring up her death. She wouldn't use that word; she would say "when it happens" or something along those lines. She made sure that I knew she had added me to bank accounts and the deed to the house and that I knew her final wishes.

One day when I was visiting from Iowa, she mentioned what she wanted at her funeral. We decided I would do her eulogy. Mother wanted a white casket, adding quite seriously, "But nothing cheap." I still chuckle at that.

During Mother's last year or so I arranged for caregivers to come and do what was needed to help her at home. My objective was to keep in her home for as long as possible. I knew she did not want to go to a care facility at any time for any reason. Professional caregivers, women who were members of a former Baptist church we attended for many years, came to the home and provided assistance, cooking, cleaning, monitoring her health, sitting with her. In her final months, that became 24 hours a day.

My last visit with her was early in January, 2006. I knew a final change was coming; I *felt* it during that last visit. There was a heaviness in my spirit the entire visit. One afternoon I tried to escape to a movie theater: it was a film about country music legend Johnny Cash. I could not concentrate. I could not finish the movie.

I wept.

I tried getting a bite to eat, cheeseburgers continuing to be a favorite, and I stopped for a Sonic burger, but that didn't do it.

I couldn't finish the burger; the taste just wasn't there.

On Tuesday I needed to catch an afternoon flight back to Iowa. Mother had been lying in her bed but a caregiver prepared her lunch. She sat down at the head of her dining room table, nibbling at her food. I knew it. There wasn't much more that could be said. Time was slipping away.

I stood up from my chair, "Well Mother, I am going to head out to the airport," I said slowly as I looked at her, worn and weary, her tired eyes looking at her plate.

"I love you," were my last words to the woman who gave me everything she could, who gave me the best she could offer. As I bent down to kiss her on her forehead Mother whispered her last words to me. "I love you too."

Less than a week later, on the following January Monday morning, in the presence of one of her dedicated caregivers, Mother answered the final eternal call of her name. *Ellen, come on home.*

Mother lived a full, good life and did her best with what God gave her.

Thank you, Mother, for everything. With Love.

Sis. Ellen Jarrell,
A Woman of God's Understanding you are the wisest. You taught so many to press on as well as myself. God did not say it would be easy, but through it all he has made you strong and unmovable. God is not done with you yet. Keep pressing on toward the mark of a higher calling. His grace is sufficient for you. God has put in you a great work, and he will perform it until the day of Jesus Christ.

Mother Ellen Jarrell

Wanda and her grandchildren at Mother's funeral in 2006

Ellen and Fred Jarrell, 1981

CHAPTER 5
Gentle, Sweet Nudging

I've noted that it was the birth of my children that rekindled the fires of my curiosity regarding my biological father. That missing part of my background began to loom large. How could I attempt to help them prepare for their futures if I didn't have a handle on my own past? How could I face their questions if I had made no attempt to find answers to my own?

It was my daughter Regina, as she grew from teenager to young adult, who posed the probing question: "Will you ever try to contact your dad again?"

"Someday I will" or "one of these days" were my usual responses.

They were honest replies. I wanted to feel comfortable knowing that if and when I was successful in my pursuit, I would have no regrets. The journey, I clearly understood, would be an emotional rollercoaster.

It was all about timing, which included my being comfortable with who I was, understanding that revelations about my biological father would, of course, lead to new discoveries about myself and reawaken buried truths, faults, and weaknesses.

Regina's gentle inquiries kept the issue on my mind. I've always appreciated her unique way of thinking, from her artist's eye, her vibrant, colorful perceptions of life. Her inquiries were never threatening, judgmental, or accusatory. They were just attempts to find out more about me and in turn help her discover who she was and her family roots. To paraphrase a famous quote, "How can you know where you are going if you don't know where you've been?"

Daughter Regina

CHAPTER 6
Little People

Little people are intriguing, enlightening, and loving blessings from God. They are human tape recorders sure to repeat or mimic behavior they have seen or heard. They are also teachers of and for themselves, other children, and, most importantly, adults.

Our son Julian bears a strong resemblance to me.

Jonathan exhibits a number of physical characteristics from his mother's family, especially his mother and her younger brother, Elvyn, aka Skeet.

And Regina from her birth to this day bears a strong resemblance to her older brother Julian.

Our children at Christmas in Davenport, IA

Julian, Regina and Jonathan in New York City, 2009

Canetha and our boys, Julian and Jonathan

But who do I look like?

In some ways I clearly have some of Wanda's physical traits but have other physical characteristics that must come from the other side of my family tree.

What kind of tree is it? Oak? Elm? Does the tree stand strong and tall, courageous in strength, elegant in its height? Is it a productive fruit-bearing tree producing apples, pears, lemons?

Or is it a broken, worn, weathered tree, its branches and limbs dying, its trunk bearing scars of abuse and neglect, its fruit rotten and decaying?

These were questions I needed to answer to feel complete. They had burrowed themselves deep into my subconscious. I needed to know, I needed to discover, I needed to experience and, if at all possible, I needed to *see* this man who was my biological father. Eyes meeting, face-to-face, man to man.

But after all these years, was he still alive? If so, where? In what condition? And if he was alive and healthy, would he even acknowledge my presence?

I took nothing for granted but kept hope alive that even if my attempts to locate him proved futile, at least I would see a photograph of Myron Clay, before I died.

Most people can't truly understand and many may never truly identify with this intense need to "see" a parent. Perhaps it's a part of their lives most folks take for granted; they know who their parents are and what they look like. They grew up in the home with one or both parents or, like me, they were raised by other relatives and had some knowledge of who their parents were. Yet there are many people like me who know part of their family heritage but feel incomplete because another part of their family history is hidden, the details known only by an intimate few who are not sharing them.

For years the question lingered: *What does Myron look like?* Yes, it was most certainly a big deal. I longed to know just a few of the details.

Wanda clearly did not want to talk about it, and Mother didn't know. Mother told me what she had been told, but that wasn't much.

"One time he came over to Wanda's house while you were in Kansas City drunk and wanting to see you, but Wanda ran him off." That was all she said. That one sentence told me that he knew where Wanda lived, knew about me, wanted to see me, lived in KC, had a drinking problem, and could be intimidated by a short spitfire of a woman. For years that was all I had to go on.

Once, during the late 1990's, one of Wanda's younger sisters, Deniece, said she was in a KC store when Myron approached and spoke to her. She recognized him and they exchanged brief pleasantries. Apparently that was the extent of their conversation, but at least she told me. At least, I knew that at that time he was still alive and apparently living in KC. Deniece, although willing, couldn't answer many of my questions. And I did not make any inquiries to any of Wanda's other siblings. Wanda was the oldest of Red Boy's children and his only child with Rosie Lee. I didn't know if her siblings knew Myron, but I always felt, at least while Wanda was alive, that questions about him should be addressed to her.

It was all a tightly woven mystery. Regardless, I held onto the faith and hope that one day this, agonizing mystery of my life would be solved before it was too late.

CHAPTER 7
Questions

Is this all there is to life?

I was adopted, growing up in a household as an only child. It was not as great as it may appear. Actually, I would not wish that situation on any child. Certainly there were highs, being the center of attention, experiencing joy and unconditional love. But there were lows, too. And they were harsh and soul searing.

There was frustration. Anxiety. Stark loneliness.

Sometimes it was emotionally painful, especially as a teenager. Waking in the middle of the night, staring at the four walls of my bedroom, I wondered *Is this all there is to life?*

A lot of folks just simply don't understand. Unless you have lived it.

Having to do a lot of things by yourself. Having to play by yourself. Facing challenges and hard choices, by yourself. Dealing with peer pressure, adult and child bullying – the list goes on. By yourself.

Being stabbed in the back by so-called friends, learning to deal with it, by yourself.

Nasty, harsh comments from adults, sometimes even from relatives. Learning to deal with negative people and situations too often, by yourself.

Will things ever change? Will I ever change?

There were supportive relatives and spaces. Aunt Nan's and Uncle Penney's house on Erie, with their children was my second home. Dropped off there to play with the cousins, their home was place of refuge. Now I know it was "babysitting," but then I saw it as companionship.

Or trips to Oklahoma City to visit cousin Tracy, whose mother Aunt Rosetta was Mother's sister. Another home away from home. At Aunt Ruth's, Mother's sister in Oklahoma City, Tracy and I would dance, dance, dance to James Brown, "I Feel Good!", or the tunes of The Temptations, Supremes, and the Motown sound.

Then there was Mother's sister Aunt Jessie and her husband Uncle Lucious, and their farm just outside of Eufaula, a special place in the country enveloped with love and kindness. There were many others, people and places that served as oases of happiness and joy, an escape from the harsh reality of feeling both alone and lonely. But being in a household as an only child was tough. Period.

Then as I got older I realized that not only did I have to deal with the suffocating emotions of loneliness, but that there was so much I didn't even know about myself.

As I became an adult and began to expand my interests and develop my goals, the question lingered.

Who am I?

Sometimes endless questions swamped my mind. It was like attempting to fill a void, trying to fill in an incomplete picture of myself. There would be times when hardly any thoughts would come to mind regarding this mystery man, my birthfather.

Either way, I still felt incomplete.

Most people who are not adopted have little idea what being adopted feels like. I've heard of and known adoptees who say they have little or no interest in knowing who their biological parents are, that they are perfectly content with the people they know as parents and they are satisfied with their lives.

However, even if such persons don't care to know, even if they profess to be satisfied, I still believe that at some point they have either had or will have questions. And those unanswered questions don't just simply evaporate into the abyss. Questions are borne from natural curiosity, prompted perhaps by a glance in the mirror, a personality characteristic, a biological trait, or subconscious quirk. For example: I don't like my food touching on the plate, although I've gotten a little better tolerating this as I've grown older.

Add that to being called a "picky" or "finicky" eater (I prefer terms such as selective or even discriminating). I remember at many a family holiday dinner my eating idiosyncrasies were duly noted by an observant relative.

Is that just me or was there someone in my unknown family background with such a tendency?

Since childhood I've been plagued with headaches. Mother read someplace that drinking coffee could help soothe headaches. Thus she allowed me to drink coffee at an early age.

I remember Grandpa Tom Jones warning that "Drinking coffee will make you black."

That didn't scare me; it didn't matter. Anything to help with the headaches.

For years I'd heard about Grandmother Rosie Lee's problem with headaches and her death in her early thirties. But what about the other side of my family? What health concerns or issues were there on my biological father's side?

That unknown biological parent was still very much a part of who I was; to deny that was to deny part of myself.

CHAPTER 8
Memories

Pop never took me to a basketball, football, baseball or any other kind of game or sports event, although he attended my track meets. Whether it was a drive-in or indoor theater, Pop did not take me to see a movie. He never attended a parent-teacher conference at Ingalls elementary, Mayberry Junior High or Wichita West High School.

Pop never read a story to me from a book or magazine, although he would sing a ditty which he probably made up called "Diddy, Diddy" at bedtime when I was small.

Although he never took me camping or fishing, when I was elementary school age, he took me hunting and taught me to shoot. Armed with a .22 caliber rifle I became a pretty good shot.

Regardless of all the things that Pop might not have done, one thing is crystal clear. I never doubted that Pop loved me. No, he never said it, but I knew it. Perhaps there were a number of things that other fathers may have done that he didn't, but there is a long list of things too numerous to write that he did.

What I thought was a creek a few blocks from the house was actually a drainage canal that ran parallel to McAdams Park. That small body of water, with toads, frogs, and small fish was just a fun play area. I'd play in the water, catch critters under Pop's watchful eye, and bring home all kinds of natural treasures. Of course, my pants and shoes would be soaking wet and caked with dark, smelly mud but I had too much fun in what I thought was my own private water park. Mother was not happy about my watery exploits, but that didn't stop Pop from taking me there. I don't know what I enjoyed most, being in the water or spending that play time with Pop.

No, he never got in the water but also never tempered my enthusiasm for this time and place.

Then there were the hunting sessions. In dead of winter, snow a foot deep or more, often with Uncle Ruester (who took me to my first semi-professional baseball game) we would go in search of small game, rabbits, and squirrels, out in "the country." Sometimes we were successful, sometimes not. Pop used a shotgun and, while he taught me how to shoot, Pop didn't like to waste shells or bullets. Consequently, I got a couple of BB rifles and continued my hunting for sparrows and robins in the huge old tree that was in the backyard of our house.

Although my aim became quite accurate, hunting was not one of my favorite pastimes. I did not like killing things. I came to see those small animals and birds as God's creatures and began to appreciate all of God's creation and the majesty of his handiwork. I understand that some people hunt for food and I have no problem with that, but hunting and killing just for sport became repulsive to me.

Something else garnered my attention: learning to drive.

One of my fondest memories involves Pop's old work car and bright, clear, sunny Sunday afternoon drives in the country. That's when I learned to drive before my feet could even reach the pedals. I was in third or fourth grade when he started teaching me to drive his work car. It was a two-tone, brown and white 1950's era Chevy Bel Air.

"Can I drive today?" would be my question, and we'd pile into the car. He'd drive through the city to a particular country gravel and dirt road north of town. It was always a Sunday afternoon and only during pleasant weather. I'd sit on his lap and turn the steering wheel while he operated the floor pedals. Later I sat on a pillow and operated the wheel and the foot pedals. I would drive this winding, twisting road until we reached a particular spot where it intersected with a main street or highway. Then we would turn around and I would drive back to our starting place, leaving plenty of time for me to get my drive in. I looked forward to those driving sessions. Not only was it fun but I felt *pretty special* learning how to drive at that age.

One memorable moment happened when I was either in fourth or fifth grade. I was on the school safety patrol, a group of students who were given small stop signs mounted on four- to five-foot poles and who served as crossing guards at several of the elementary school intersections. There were generally four or five boys at each intersection.

One particular sunny afternoon Pop picked me up after patrol. What he did next surprised me: he slid over for me to drive home. Grabbing the pillow, I slid under the steering wheel. My head was barely over the top of the wheel. In front of the other boys on patrol, I drove the four blocks home! I marveled at their shock and felt exhilarated and full of pride at that moment. Pop gave me an incredible gift that day and I felt on top of the world. Of course, I clearly understand now the legal and even possible tragic consequences of that decision, but there was no traffic, he was close by, and we had done this before on a country road on those Sunday afternoons.

Reggie leaning against Mother's 1965 Oldsmobile

Some relatives would tease Pop at the chance he was taking.
"If Fred is ever caught, they will put him *under* the jail." It wasn't that he didn't care. If he didn't think I could do it safely and successfully, he would not have allowed me to drive. Pop knew exactly what he was doing. Besides, we never got caught. And there were never any close calls, no accidents or confrontations with the police. So by the time I was twelve or thirteen, I had become quite comfortable with driving.
Thanks, Pop.

Unfortunately, I couldn't replicate the learning to drive sessions with my children as I was a practicing lawyer at the time. I did take Regina, when she was high school, for a few driving sessions when I was no longer practicing law.

I've always greatly appreciated what Pop did, not only because he taught me how to drive, but also because of his confidence in my ability. His mantra was "always watch out for the other guy." Pop's display of trust in me was wonderful for this little boy's confidence and self-esteem.

Our three-member family was not touchy-feely like some families are, hugging and kissing upon greeting, introduction, or leaving. But there was one standout moment that exhibited Pop's compassion and understanding.

Her name was Colleen and she was the longtime girlfriend of one of my track buddies, Willie. Willie and I were among a group of sprinters on the mid-1970's West High School track team. We were also participants in various record breaking and championship relay teams. Colleen and Willie were juniors when we met, and I was a sophomore. Members of the track team, and their girlfriends formed a close-knit bond.

Colleen and I sat near each other at the rear of our science class, which was taught by a very kind gentleman, Mr. Haynes. We had conversations that broached all kinds of subjects before, in between, and after class. Some of those conversations were heart wrenching.

Colleen was short and heavy set with long dark hair and penetrating green eyes. She was also Caucasian, and that made their relationship somewhat challenging as Willie was Black.

Colleen told me they had plans to marry, but some members of her family were prejudiced and opposed their relationship. Sometimes their bigotry manifested itself in very hurtful comments and behavior. Regardless Colleen was determined to have a future with Willie and Willie felt the same about Colleen.

Generally when you saw one, the other was nearby.

Several months into the fall of their senior year, 1973. Colleen had gotten a small compact car, a Chevrolet Vega, I believe.

At that time the school sometimes rented a local movie theater and actually dismissed school so students could see a particular film. It may have been some type of fundraiser and students had to find their own transportation to the theater. There was no bus service. Thus those who went either drove or caught rides to the popular, modern theater, located in the Twin Lakes shopping mall several miles from West High.

On this particular gloomy, rainy, morning, October 9, 1973, I remember pulling behind Willie on 21st Street. We were stopped by a train as we were on the way to the movie theater.

"Where's Colleen," I asked Willie as we both got out of our cars. "She's on her way," Willie replied. "She will meet me there."

The train crossed and we were back in our cars, on our way.

The rain had stopped.

Upon arriving at the packed theater and being seated, before the lights went down, I remember seeing Willie walk up and down the aisles.

Willie's looking for Colleen, I thought. *I wonder where she is.* From where I was sitting, toward the back, it did not appear he found her.

The movie finished and we returned to West.

Sometime later that day, I heard that Colleen and two other female friends, earlier that morning while traveling those rain slick streets, were in a horrible three car accident on the way to the theater. The two friends suffered various injuries but Colleen didn't make it. Colleen, at seventeen, was gone.

That knowledge was beyond our youthful comprehension and shock and anguish took over our hearts. This quiet, unassuming, compassionate, understanding, caring teenager was gone. Willie was in a daze.

Several days later I went to the funeral. There Colleen lay in her casket dressed in a lovely pink chiffon dress looking peacefully beautiful, as if she was merely asleep. No injuries from the accident showed on her face.

I held it together at the funeral and at the cemetery. But on the way home, driving alone, my grief ignited. I held it in check until I arrived home and went into our small kitchen. Pop joined me, standing in front of the kitchen sink.

Then, after several days of putting on the strong face, I erupted into heavy sobs and an avalanche of tears. My spirit broke.

Pop didn't say a word. He took me into his arms and held me like a child awakening from a terrible nightmare. I told him about Colleen and the agonizing and difficult times I knew she had gone through. I had seen how much in love she was with Willie, how unfairly and wrongly some people, including her family, had treated her. Still, she had continued to believe the best of people, hoping that things would be better some day, that she would experience joy and happiness without interference or interruption.

During that moment, in the kitchen, time stood still as Pop held me and I wept. I was as tall as Pop was, perhaps a bit taller, but there we stood, a father comforting his devastated son who had experienced the death of a friend.

After a while I regained my composure, cleared my eyes, and dried my tear-stained face. Pop never said a word then or afterwards. We never spoke of that moment. But I remember and treasure the memory. That was Pop, a strong, silent man full of compassion, understanding, and love.

It's been decades since Pop's death, but I still miss his wide grin, his hearty laugh, the gleam in his eyes. Regina was born two years after Pop's death and my grown sons are now older than I was when he died. We adjust, we move forward, and life goes on, but that void remains. Pop will never be replaced.

CHAPTER 9
Research

My initial research to locate my biological father was done the old fashioned way, via telephone books, city directories, etc. This was before the advent of the internet, web pages, and instant access to information. It was slow searching by fingertips. Kansas City phone books and directories had provided an address years earlier, in 1983 or '84, and I had written Myron Clay a letter from New Orleans.

By the mid-2000's, while we were living in Davenport, I was searching via the internet. I found several Myron Clays, located from the Kansas City area to Michigan.

Which one was my Myron Clay?

Once I asked Wanda and she didn't know, at least that was what she said at the time. "I'll ask Tina to look," she said referring to her daughter, my sister. "She works for the utility company," and she could probably find out.

Nothing ever came of that. I continued to get the impression that Wanda still really didn't want to talk about Myron. However, my research produced valuable bits of information. I discovered the names of his parents: his mother Odessa and father, also named Myron, who served in the military and is buried in a Kansas military cemetery. I later learned he was referred to as "Big Myron." Subsequently I found the obituary and funeral information of Myron's only brother Ronell Clay.

With the internet I was able to amass somewhat detailed information about Myron — where he lived, what property he owned, his favorite automotive type (Cadillac), and the record of his payment of property taxes.

I organized a "Myron" file and would add bits and pieces of information as I gathered them. I viewed this as similar to putting the pieces of a puzzle together, yet this puzzle consisted of secrets and mysteries of *my life*. I was in for quite a ride, one which would exceed my wildest dreams and expectations.

CHAPTER 10
Decisions (Seminary)

By early 2002, I had experienced most of the responsibilities of Baptist ministry: baptism, communion, hospital and home visitation, and a brief stint as an Interim Pastor. This was in addition to serving as a church deacon and Sunday School teacher on a rotation basis with both adults and junior children.

After my term as Interim Pastor at the Progressive Baptist Church and more than a decade of ministry I was led by the Holy Spirit to the First Baptist Church, in Davenport. The character, environment, and demographics of First Baptist (traditional, primary Caucasian and senior citizen with some diversity) was vastly different from that of Progressive (contemporary, predominately African American with a wide range of age groups).

By 2004, I had preached First Baptist Church several times and had become a member of that wonderful congregation. While the church was seeking an interim pastor I had been asked to fill in as "pulpit supply," meaning bringing weekly sermons. This did not require any administrative or managerial duties.

By 2004, a wonderful married couple, Drs. Maynard and Ruth Hatch, were filling the position of interim pastors while the church searched for a permanent leader. One Sunday afternoon after service Dr. Maynard Hatch spoke to me.

"Reggie, You should consider going to seminary. There is money out there."

He caught me off guard, as his statement came completely out of the blue. I knew of a few other black Baptist ministers who had gone to seminaries, but I had never entertained the thought. And at the time there was a lot going on in my life.

My sons were both in college, Julian at New York University and Jonathan at Tulane University. Regina was in high school. Mother was sick, and I also had some lingering, long term health issues.

In addition, I had promised myself after finishing law school in 1987 that I was done with going to school, no more formal, structured educational programs for me.

No, no, no! I thought. I had already done just about everything in ministry. Why did I need to go to seminary? *I just don't see the need,* I mused.

I didn't say that to Dr. Hatch at the time. I just nodded and indicated I would give it some consideration.

And I gave it some, very brief consideration and dismissed it. For a while, a long while. But that wonderful Christian preacher had planted the seed.

When Dr. Hatch first made the suggestion, I was practicing law as an assistant public defender. While our office had a very liberal, understanding and progressive supervisor, the work itself could be trying and stressful. The task as a court appointed attorney was to provide legal representation to people accused of committing crimes.

And some people made it clear they did not want a public defender but "a *paid* attorney," even if they couldn't afford one. That was the paradox, being appointed to zealously represent someone, who in turn, did not want your help. Their resistance could range from noncooperation and ignoring me to hardcore disdain and hostility. Coupled with the attitudes of some judges, some opposing prosecutors, and, on occasion, the bias and prejudice of some juries against our clients, this made for more than a few highly stressful situations.

Much was happening in my life at that time and I was applying for other jobs. Many places. All across the country. Even in Alaska and I do not like cold weather. I was doing everything I could to get out of that line of work and land another job while I had a job.

There were other considerations: the boys were at university, but Regina was still a student of the Davenport public school system and I really didn't want to uproot her, if possible. She had done very well and was involved in many activities. Moving, finding a new residence, a new community, new school, new routine, new friends, would pose enough challenges for her.

My going back to school was simply out of the question. Relocation for a job, yes, for school, no. An adamant No.

At the time I also was encouraging other members of my family to consider continuing their education. My wife Canetha had earned an Associate of Arts degree but hadn't considered a Bachelor's degree. The boys were still college undergraduates, but I emphasized the need for them to think about graduate degrees. Regina we wanted to go to college. I have always been pro-education, believing the more education one has the better prepared one is for whatever life presents (or throws at you).

And in 2004, I had finally had surgery for a long term, lingering illness regarding my esophagus and stomach that had greatly impacted my life for many years. It was a dreadful, nasty illness that it took years for doctors and specialists to finally diagnose and treat. It also required many months of battling with an insurance company over choice of doctors and health coverage.

I constantly meditated and prayed on what, when, and how to do next. So much was on the table. Mother was sick in Wichita with cancer, diabetes, among health issues, and I was going back and forth home to check on her, along with monitoring the home health care workers from 500 miles plus away.

How could I even consider returning to school, even if I wanted to?

Slowly things settled down.

The year 2006 was a turning point. That early fall, Canetha and I celebrated twenty-five years of marriage with a trip to Europe, the long overdue "honeymoon" we never had. The boys graduated college. Mother died. Regina finished high school. I even changed jobs, but what I thought was going to be an ideal situation, returning to journalism, turned out to be again very trying, stressful, and dreadful. I was praying before going to work every day that I would just make it through the day.

I had returned to journalism with the Moline Dispatch Publishing Company as primarily a features reporter. I had hoped that would be a long-term stay and envisioned buying a house in rural Rock Island or Henry County with a few acres of land and writing (books) on the side. This was going to be it.

Not.

One must be careful about trying to repeat job experiences: it may be the same place, with many of the same people, in the same positions as previously employed, but this situation was indeed different.

The newspaper experience, after a bright, refreshing start, turned stale and sour. It became one of my worst employment experiences, despite my earnest prayers. But God answered my lamentations once again in unexpected ways.

I began to meet people who, in some way or another, fanned the fires of my interest in seminary. Perhaps they were angels?

Once, again, stress, pressure, health issues all combined to produce an internal flashing message, "Time to Go! Time to Go!"

Not only did my wife note the effect on my health but my long time, very efficient, very capable doctor advised me to look for something else. And I did.

But too much was going on for me to go to seminary. Then, as Mother often said, "time brings about a change." And it did.

One of the sources I developed at the newspaper was the director of a local men's homeless shelter, operated by a nonprofit Christian organization. The director, Gary, became a valuable source for stories. Most importantly, Gary served as another one of God's unlikely messengers to me. Gary had a seminary degree, but before he learned of my ministerial background (and after we had developed a professional reporter/source relationship), he made another one of those *Moses and the burning bush/Paul Damascus road* statements:

"Reggie, you should go to seminary," Gary advised. "It would be good for you."

Up to that point we had talked religion and Christianity but nothing ever bordered on the topic of seminary. The man didn't even know that I was a preacher!

Then one of the shelter's transient clients provided another "sign." Men could only stay in the homeless shelter for a specific period of time. There were several structured programs to help clients get back on their feet.

By this time Gary had learned I was a minister and sometimes after work I would go to the men's shelter and bring a short message, a sermonette, before dinner. I did this several times and received unexpected blessings from this experience.

On one occasion a tall, lanky, middle aged Caucasian man with long, blond mussed hair and a beard caught my attention. He was missing several front teeth and had faced numerous life battles. His jeans and shirt were tattered and worn. In the 1960's he would have been described as a hippie.

I'd brought the message that evening to the group of about 20 men, and they were lining up to pass through the dinner line. There was an upright piano in the small dining area with the top closed.

I saw this straggly, gap-toothed homeless man sit down at the piano.

Is he going to tap out a few minor notes or something? I thought. Then the man began to play and I was shocked.

He can tickle those ivories! He made that piano sing! This stranger played the piano gospel style, "Precious Lord" and "Amazing Grace" rendered, as well as any professional pianist in a Black church *anywhere*. Looking at his appearance, reading only his cover, one would never guess the talent and skill he possessed.

He didn't play for long, as the director told him to shut it down, but not before gaining my undivided attention and preparing me for yet another message.

Afterward the man asked me for a ride, just a few blocks. I rarely give rides to strangers but this time I did. During that ride I learned that he was a professional musician, but he said something else that I interpreted as another sign. He volunteered that he had attended seminary, didn't have his degree, but needed to go pick it up.

He brought up the word, seminary.

That word just kept coming up, no escaping it. Slowly the message began to sink in. In some ways I'd hit rock bottom, there was nowhere to go but up. I couldn't pick myself up, I simply didn't know what to do or how to do. Yet it became clear the answer was not changing jobs but receiving further education.

I finally "got" the message.

I had started at some point during my job search sending for information regarding seminaries. Just inquiries, nothing serious. Now I would check into it. Seriously.

I sought seminaries and divinity schools affiliated with the American Baptist denomination, the affiliation of First Baptist Church in Davenport. After all my investigation I was inspired to apply to only one seminary: While there was a seminary in Dubuque, Iowa less than 75 miles away, I could not see myself either living in that community or commuting to school. In addition, it was not Baptist and although I did visit that seminary, attending a class and finding the people pleasant, it wasn't quite the fit I was looking for.

All the signs pointed to the American Baptist Seminary of the West (ABSW), now called The Berkeley School of Theology. Usually in applying to colleges or graduate schools, I would apply to multiple programs. Not now. I applied only to ABSW.

I had been to Berkeley once, in 1991 or 1992 as part of a lawyer training program for a three- or four-day workshop and retained fond memories of this event held at the University of California Berkeley law school.

I had to submit all of the supporting documents: transcripts, references, etc. as well as money for the application itself, on campus housing deposit. Due to my very tight financial circumstances and the logistics of contacting my prior schools for transcripts and paying those fees, the amazing thing was that despite many of those documents being submitted after posted deadlines, ABSW accepted my materials.

God's hand just seemed to be in this from day one.

So many things had to fall into place, chief among them, Canetha needed to be comfortable with the fact I would be across the country in school while she lived on her own nearly 2,000 miles away. Despite the challenges, I knew that she would be all right.

ABSW offered several advantages: although the student enrollment figures were small, there was a strong African America presence and tradition at this seminary. Several present or past administrators and/or professors were African American.

It was important, after all of my prior educational experiences, to be in an academic environment that not only acknowledged but respected the African American religious and spiritual experience. I had been in some situations, both as student and teacher, where that, unfortunately, was not the case. In too many instances I was the only African American student in the class, or even the program. Far too often I felt *invisible*, as writer Ralph Ellison so accurately and eloquently described in his novel *Invisible Man*.

I sought a seminary education not to pastor, not to become a chaplain or missionary, but to become a more effective minister, whatever form my ministry might take. I wanted to be a better communicator and to simply know more about the Bible, God, Christianity, and myself.

In the spring of 2008 things slowly fell into place, sometimes literally at the very last moment. It also became clear it was going to take all of my financial resources, and then some, for this to happen. To return to school nearly 2,000 miles away in California I was going to have to risk, if not give up, everything—job, retirement and/or pension accounts, leaving home, family, and friends, everything.
This was an exercise in faith.

Other concerns were my health. I've recounted my health issues earlier but I also suffered from Hypertension, an effect of stress. In addition, sometimes it seems that I could not half remember what I had for lunch a few days ago, so how would I ever remember enough to pass seminary tests? Then there was the age element: I entered law school decades ago, in my mid- to late-20's, still a young man. Entering seminary full time, I was in my early 50's and all kinds of things in life had changed.

Why Lord?

God's ways, thoughts and plans are truly known only to God.

It's up to us to fall in line, fall in place, through faith.

And so I did, the best way I knew how. In faith.

After all of the paperwork had been submitted, began the waiting game. Waiting to hear about admission and financial aid. I was wary of additional student loans as I was still paying off my law school debt. But I was willing to do whatever was necessary.

Finally, the news.

Canetha was working the evening shift in the women's wear department at J.C. Penney's and stood at the register without customers. I approached her with the news.

"I got in!" I was excited but still exercising caution. "I don't know if I'm going, but at least I got in." Canetha was glad but also somewhat reserved, and I saw in her eyes that, despite my reservations and cautionary musings, she knew if I was in, I was going. Somehow. Someway. It was going to happen.

And it did.

Seminary was essential in so many ways to my emotional, mental, and spiritual growth.

Wanda understood my situation and despite the challenges was, as usual, encouraging. "I hope it works out," she said, emphasizing holding onto faith about the decision.

This experience was also vital in my quest to know more about God and myself. And to know myself I needed to know more about my father.

I had to find Myron.

CHAPTER 11
The Journey

Lord, I cannot do this alone!

Sun rays pounded the pavement the late August day Regina and I pulled away from the curb from our Davenport home and headed for California. The PT Cruiser was packed to the moon roof with her things needed for her sophomore year at the University of San Francisco and with mine as well.

We left home and drove one block west on our red brick street to our first stop sign. As I pulled to a stop, reality slapped me in the face: I am on my way to California and there's no going back. In that brief moment I was on the verge of feeling overwhelmed at the monumental change that was taking place.

Lord, how am I going to do this? I cannot do this alone!

We have so far to go.

Not only was this a physical journey across freeways and interstate highways, 2,000 miles across plains and mountains, it was an emotional and spiritual journey as well. The significance was not lost on me.

It was definitely a new chapter.

Wife Canetha was a trooper. I had done my best to prepare her for this transition as so much was literally up in the air until the last moment. Specifically, if I was really going to make this happen, it would require all of my financial resources, and more, and so many things had to fall into place, like student housing on campus.

Although it was not a mutual decision that I go off to seminary, it was something I felt called to do. Some things I knew Canetha would not understand. I just believed that God would work things out if I did the best that I could in planning and stepping out on faith. Like my call to ministry in 1991, this decision was a long time in the making.

Canetha and Reggie's Wedding 1981

Jarrell Family

Canetha and Reggie in Switzerland for their 25th anniversary, 2006

Although it was not a mutual decision that I go off to seminary, it was something I felt called to do. Some things I knew Canetha would not understand. I just believed that God would work things out if I did the best that I could in planning and stepping out on faith. Like my call to ministry in 1991, this decision was a long time in the making.

Canetha would later share her feelings about my leaving, but my plan was to eventually move her to California, although I did not share that with her, knowing that would be another issue of worry for her.

So Canetha stayed behind. But I knew she would be all right.

Once again I was traveling into the unknown with nothing taken for granted. My faith was strong and my hope intact as it was clear to me that the Holy Spirit was leading me, but still...

Emotion kicked in. It was far from clear how I would manage. Reality composed a picture that was gray, murky, and riddled with alarming streaks.

I felt trepidation that moment at that stop sign. Yet not regret. I believed God had a plan and I was going to be obedient with this giant leap of faith that took everything I had and more. And absolutely nothing was guaranteed with one exception, God's promise that He/She would not leave or forsake us.

We made the long drive to California without incident and enrolled in our respective schools. When I teased about possibly making frequent visits to Regina's campus to check on her, my beautiful, witty daughter, never at a loss for words, replied succinctly: "You stay on *your* campus and I'll stay on *mine.*"

I still chuckle at the boundaries drawn by my youngest child.

School work and the search for a job consumed me. I thought it essential that I produce some income to supplement all of my student loans. I did everything I could think of to gain employment, but that didn't happen.

It was probably for the best that I couldn't find a job, as theological study was stimulating but challenging. To have professors who knew their stuff yet were friendly and very approachable made a world of difference at this stage of my life. And this was a seminary people where were clear about their faith and comfortable expressing their beliefs.

Prayer was an essential component in some classes and at times, during prayers, singing, or preaching, the Holy Spirit was clearly felt. Frequently in or after class I felt moved by something that was said or done. In all my years of education this was a new experience. It was what I had hoped for, a graduate school with sometimes difficult issues or subjects, with prayer, faith, and belief all active components of this educational experience. I began to understand why my Rock Island friend Gary had suggested that seminary would be good for me. It made me examine myself. In that close, intense review once again the question of my father arose.

And self-examination brought up other life changing incidents stored within me, especially Wanda's health challenges from 1996-2008. Thinking of her and those final years of her life, realizing what she had gone through, again I thought of Myron. *Was he still living? What condition was he in? Would he remember me?*

My seminary experiences and self-examination led me to the conclusion that I needed to intensify my efforts to discover answers to my long-held questions about my biological father. And time was of the essence as life could change suddenly, unexpectedly.

This is the time. This is the time to act. At least try to reconnect.

My goal: was to at least, see a picture of Myron Clay, at whatever age. I thought that would satisfy me.

I could not fathom what God was going to do.

CHAPTER 12
The Letter

While in seminary in California from time to time I would return home to Davenport and sometimes travel to Kansas City. Wanda was having some serious health issues, but she was at home though she could not be alone. Tina's daughter Danielle was living with her.

In 2009, during one such visit with Wanda, after much prayer and reflection, I decided to visit the Kansas City address I had located for Myron, which wasn't far from Wanda's home.

Give it a shot, you never know.

The house sat facing the south side of the rather busy street. I drove by once or twice, having second thoughts about making this out of the blue house call. I mentally imagined several possibilities.

Hello, are you Mr. Clay? I'm Reggie Jarrell, Wanda Grant's son. How are you?

Hello, is Mr. Clay home? I would like to talk to him please. Who am I? I am ...

Hello, is your grandfather here?

Every possibility had someone answering the door.

I pulled into the driveway, in front of the two-car garage. There really wasn't any on-street parking. Nearby was a small child's basketball goal.

Slowly I walked up the steps to the small porch of the tidy, well-kept ranch-style home. I rang the doorbell, knocked on the door. No answer. I tried again.

No answer, but someone moved a front curtain and peeped out the window.

I couldn't see clearly but I got the strong impression it was a youngster. I didn't expect a child to open the door and decided to leave.

The result was not quite what I hoped or expected. Back to Wanda's to reassess what happened and what to do next. I would make no return trips to this address.

Back in Davenport when I told Canetha what happened, she suggested I write another letter.

I had a couple of possible addresses and pondered that idea, then returned to California, back to seminary. Back to my questions.

If I wrote, *What should I say?* How much information should I include? What do I not write?

I prayed. And I wrote. It's my habit to do several drafts of letters of any importance. Put it all out there, lay it on the line, and then edit. Trim and cut. Rephrase and rewrite. Then edit some more.

Finally I arrived at something I felt comfortable with. I needed to apologize for my not following up his letter of many years ago. That was wrong. He had been kind enough to not only respond to my first letter but to respond positively. Kindly.

What would his response be now after decades of not hearing from me? Would he still acknowledge me?

And those questions could be moot if Myron was dead, incapacitated, or impaired so that he couldn't respond. Like Wanda's condition.

Had I waited too long? Was it too late?

I finished my letter and with prayer mailed it to the house that I had visited.

My back up plan was to send a second letter to another address after a reasonable period of time, say thirty days, if I didn't receive a reply.

No response arrived to my letter. I revised and edited a second letter and deposited it in the mail to an address in a Kansas City suburb, Raytown, Missouri.

Shortly afterwards I had a conversation with Wanda.

"Myron got your letter," she said rather emotionlessly. I had not told her I had written.

"Oh, he did?"

"I have his number someplace, but I can't find it now. I'll let you know when I find it."

Great news! Mission accomplished! After all of these years! He is alive and well enough to write a reply! I didn't doubt Wanda, but I also understood her medical, mental, and emotional condition. I was not going to wait for her to try to locate his phone number, recalling years when she indicated she didn't know where he was, if he was alive. I didn't press her. Yet I knew what next steps I must take.

When Myron again responded to my letter, I knew what I had to do and didn't want to waste time. I wrote a third letter, this time including my phone number.

I went to the nearby Berkeley post office and deposited this vital piece of mail. If he had responded once, more than twenty years ago, and a second time just a few days ago, surely Myron would respond again.

I'm not making any assumptions, Lord, but thank you!

CHAPTER 13
The Phone Call

It was late summer, on the cusp of fall. It was also the start of new academic semester and the beginning of a new, highly anticipated chapter in my life.

After all these years, I was finally going to hear my biological father's voice! Something many people take for granted on a daily basis was going to be a major life highlight for me.

It happened on September 17, 2009, about 4 p.m. (Pacific Standard Time).

Oddly, I can't remember the specifics of our first phone contact! After my third letter from California, did he call and leave a message? Did I then return his phone call? Or did I just pick up the first time he called?

"I'm at a loss for words," Myron reflected. Myron's voice was deep, like the depths of a great river, wrapped in a rich, soothing cool baritone. He was articulate, knowledgeable, witty, and understanding. We talked like old friends who had missed many grand old times and some very important beginnings.

This first afternoon phone conversation also provided a glimpse of the young, troubled teenager that had attracted 13-year-old Wanda McClain. I could hear something of the street hustler he became, and began to learn about his family tree, binding roots, and expansive branches.

"You can ask me any question," Myron advised. He asked me to stop calling him Mr. Clay.

I called him Myron.

Myron was easy to engage with and to many of my questions he readily volunteered answers.

Myron stood 5'll", weighed 245 pounds, and wasn't currently married but had been with his current partner, Marilyn, "Tootsie," nearly twenty years. She was about twenty years his junior. I was older than she was. Marilyn had a daughter Varethia who Myron said he had adopted. He mentioned his former wife, Hurelene — the only woman he ever married. Hurelene and his mother, Orelia Clark Clay, hailed from Bradley, Arkansas.

Myron Clay (teen), Jr. ROTC

Myron Clay (young adult)

Myron Sr. and Orelia Clay, Reggie's paternal grandparents

For years it was rocky between Myron and Hurelene. She was the mother of two of his sons, Myron III and George, but they married and divorced three times. As a side note, the last time she divorced him, Myron read about it in a newspaper.

And there was more:

Myron had a total of eleven children, eight biological children by several different women; the others he said were "adopted." Whether that meant legal adoptions or informal he did not specify. I was the oldest and the youngest child, Ebony, was just a few years older than my daughter Regina. "I was a busy guy," Myron admitted.

His youngest daughter, Ebony, lived in Sacramento, California, about 75 miles from Berkeley! And Myron had two other daughters who also lived in the Bay area of Northern California. I'd traveled nearly 2,000 miles to discover I had two half-sisters as virtual neighbors. *My, my I never would have guessed!*

Of all the places I might have attended seminary, I was led to the place where I have siblings nearby! Months later I would meet Phyllis and have a telephone conversation with another half-sister, Myra. I connected with Ebony via email. The other siblings were Lataynia, Terri, Helene, and Myron's youngest son, Myron J.

There were so many other things I wanted to know about this man, just ordinary things such as his interests and hobbies. Across the years I'd wondered if he was an athlete or musician. If so, what sports, what instrument? Was he a professional, blue-collar worker, or one of the many who had met rather unfortunate circumstances in life and was living on the streets?

Then there was another possibility: Was Myron Clay a prisoner locked away in a cramped, iron cell somewhere never to taste freedom again in this life?

That initial phone conversation, the first of many, started to provide some answers. Myron enjoyed music, particularly jazz, but he was neither a musician nor an athlete. He loved books and was an avid reader, yet besides fiddling with his computer he had no other real hobbies. He was once a mason. One thing he did know and owned: firearms. And he kept the variety of pistols, revolvers, and shotguns he possessed all loaded. "An unloaded gun is like a car without gas. What good is it?" Myron inquired.

For years Myron carried a gun. Anywhere. Even for brief excursions, like going out of his home to get his newspaper. I asked what gun he carried most. His surprising answer was characteristic of his quick wit.

"It depended upon the outfit I was wearing." He was dead serious.

As the years rolled on Myron saw the danger of carrying a gun and stopped packing heat. "I figured if I needed to take a gun with me, I didn't need to go there."

He also realized that one could get so caught up in a moment and make a rash, impulsive decision that could end in tragedy. If a person had a gun, he rationalized, the tendency was to shoot first, ask questions later. However, if the person didn't have a gun, he would be forced to find another way to deal with the situation, even if it meant simply leaving the scene.

Maturity and wisdom transformed Myron, but it took some long years and hard times. As a teenager when he met my mother, he was preparing for a life as a hustler and doing all he could to find trouble. And find it he did. When I was born he was locked in juvenile detention for a theft-related crime. When he was released, I had already been adopted and few relatives knew the specifics. Those who did know weren't telling him. He was devastated and sought consolation from his mother.

"I cried," he said.

But he continued getting entangled in crimes. "I was a bad boy," Myron said, "in spite of the loving care of my parents." He was the oldest of three, with a brother, Ronell, and sister, Cozette. His mother, Orelia Clark, had family roots in Louisiana. She was feisty, short, and extremely bright, and could curse like a sailor. She was a LPN but worked as a RN in a black, segregated Kansas City hospital. In middle age she suffered a stroke but bounced back well enough to care for mentally ill patients in their home. She was a smoker and later died of a heart attack.

His father, "Big Myron," hailed from Warrensburg, Missouri. He served in World War II and afterwards worked for twenty-five years in Kansas City's water department. Big Myron was a smoker and died of cancer of the esophagus.

Despite the structure of home life, Myron was drawn to the songs of the Kansas City streets. He lost focus in school and dropped out in his mid-teens. When I asked what high school he attended, Myron didn't hesitate. "All of them," he said, later amending his answer to "probably only three."

Once Myron related a story that involved problems at East, an integrated Kansas City high school. Myron felt threatened by some Caucasian guys. I'm not sure if it was a general atmosphere of racial hostility and tension or if he was a target and had some difficulty with specific individuals. Regardless, Myron had a simple solution. He took a loaded pistol and kept it in his locker at school.

Thank goodness it didn't go farther than that.

Finally at his last school the principal, a Black man, had experienced enough of Myron Clay.

"I cut class and was playing dice, craps," Myron remembered.

This principal was not playing.

"You can be suspended for two weeks, or you can quit."

Myron did not take kindly to ultimatums from anyone and decided he'd had enough.

"I quit," Myron said. "My mother cried and cried. She pleaded for me not to quit, to go back to school. But I wouldn't."

Years later Myron regretted that decision and realized that was a major mistake. And he eventually realized what he wanted to be: an intellectual, an academic, and a scholar. He told me that another major regret of life was not being allowed to attend a Seventh Day Adventist school. Although that was his family's religion, his parents weren't very religious nor active in any church. To his dismay, his parents simply would not let him attend the religious school.

"Why should we pay for you to go to school when you can go to school for free," they said. Public education in Kansas City had few costs while the private religious school meant tuition, room, and board, among other expenses.

Less than one year later, after quitting school, he was incarcerated. He later earned his General Education Degree in prison.

Although Myron didn't say it, perhaps it was his parents' attitude toward his desire to attend a religious school that sparked his rebellion, attracted him to the street life. At nearly seventy-years old, his pain and disappointment still clearly showed talking about this.

Added to his fiercely independent, stubborn, and headstrong nature was his keen insight and intellect. These personality characteristics could have been forged into either positive or negative behavior. During his find-yourself teenage years, Myron opted for the latter, which led to crimes, conviction, jail, and prison.

Myron spent a total of six years, at three different time periods, in prison on burglary, robbery, and conspiracy to commit theft convictions. After his third prison term Myron changed his attitude and habits. Upon his release, he never returned to prison.

"I've been clean for 45, 46 years," he mentioned. When he got out, he was determined to stay out. With the help of a friend, a police official, Myron landed a job at Ford Motor Company where he worked some 35 years until he retired at age 60. For most of that time he worked the assembly line. A short stint as a supervisor didn't work out due to some discrimination and racism issues. A subsequent lawsuit and settlement provided a steady job and paycheck with fewer conflicts and headaches.

Easy to talk to, Myron was an engaging conversationalist with opinions on a myriad of subjects. Whether it was a quick quip or lengthy dialogue, one really never knew what was coming from Myron. Conversation certainly was never dull, dry, or boring.

That first September phone call opened a new, tantalizing chapter of my life. I was anxious to learn not only names, places, and events, but also to glimpse the mind, heart, and spirit of this strong but sensitive, quiet, sometimes withdrawn, mysterious man. And much more was to come.

CHAPTER 14
Conversations with Myron

After our first meeting in October 2009, we stayed in contact. I made a special effort to phone on some of the major holidays, especially Father's Day. We also called on each other's birthdays and I still retain on my voicemail the last two of Myron's birthday greetings: "I want to wish you a very happy birthday and many, many more."

I would visit when I had the chance. We would sit at the dining room table awhile and then move into one of the spare bedrooms that he'd turned into a small office. Black and white sketched portraits of African Americans adorned the walls. Myron would sit at his desk, home to his computer and a variety of other odds and ends, and I'd sit on a footstool. There were no other chairs in the room. And we would talk about a plethora of subjects, past, present, and future.

More than once Myron recalled the three major regrets in his life. As already mentioned, his failure to attend a Seventh Day Adventist Academy plagued him his entire life. His joy was reading and a couple of years before he died, he gave me several theological and religious treatises, some of which belonged to either his mother or grandmother. I often wondered how different his life might have been had he been allowed to pursue his educational interests during those vital, formative teen years.

His second major regret was not being able to join the armed forces. His father served in the Army in World War II, and he was interested in both the Army and Marines, applying to both services. He passed the tests for both, but first the Marines, followed by the Army rejected him. He didn't remember why the Marines rejected him, but the Army denied him because of his juvenile record.

His final regret was that he never saw me as a baby. He did not say, and I didn't ask, why he was incarcerated when I was born but he never failed to mention how he longed to hold me. He talked with his mother, who tried to comfort him, but he grieved not seeing his first child. All he knew was I was adopted. A few years later he discovered I was with relatives in Wichita, and he made plans to satisfy his long-held desire to meet me.

Somehow Myron borrowed a car and with little to no preparation, got on the road toward Wichita. He had no information, no address, no nothing, but he was determined to go to Wichita and find his son. He got a few miles on the highway and the car had mechanical problems and stopped running. On the side of the highway, his hopes dashed, he realized the futility of his plan. He returned to Kansas City and his life went on. Myron said he adopted a "hand's off," "don't rock the boat" mentality, and made no subsequent serious effort to locate me.

"I was from the wrong side of the tracks," Myron acknowledged. He felt my family viewed him as trouble.

Of course I was curious as to how he and Wanda met.

They lived in the same central city Kansas City neighborhood, within a few blocks of each other. The middle class smaller single-family homes ranged from bungalows, to ranch style homes, to two-story, traditional colonial structures. Myron lived with his family in a corner two-story home at 2400 Norton while Wanda lived with her mother, stepfather Bernard, and younger siblings at 2517 Askew. Wanda's living situation was volatile. She and her sister, Rosetta, aka Pee Wee, did not have a good relationship with their stepfather Bernard, although later in life Wanda and Bernard became close.

Just how my folks met was indeed indicative of Myron's personality.

One day Myron was just hanging out when he saw Wanda walking toward him on a sidewalk. Myron, never one to miss an opportunity to make an impression on a female, didn't simply ask for her phone number. Instead, Myron snatched her coin purse and despite her protests, refused to give it back until she relented and gave him her phone number. And that was the start of a lifelong relationship that extended through their marriages and divorces to others.

There was a time when Wanda and Myron's wife Hurelene worked for the same phone company. It was Myron's impression they knew each other. Myron emphasized that throughout the years he and Wanda always knew where the other was, what the other was doing, who the other was involved with.

That provided some clues to Wanda's reluctance over the years to talk about Myron and for me to know him. "Some things are best left in the past," she once said, which I had taken as a reference to Myron.

I came to realize, after getting to know Myron, that he was not simply a painful *past* memory for Wanda but a very real, viable, ongoing aspect of her present. He provided too many details and specifics for that to have been made up. Some of his comments filled in the gaps as to things I'd wondered about. I knew that Wanda, after her divorce from Frank, sometimes took trips, alone, just to get away, day trips, weekend jaunts, or whatever. Now I realized that she may not have always been alone. Myron implied he had been involved in some of those excursions.

That news didn't bother me at all, they were both adults. But it also became clear there was another reason that all those years Wanda didn't want to talk about Myron. Perhaps it would boil down to that she didn't want me to talk *with* Myron.

As they had been in conversation for years, Myron knew a lot about me. By the time I contacted him, Myron already knew that I was married, had three children, and knew some of the jobs I'd held.

After I had contacted Myron from California, he sent me a copy of Wanda's professional studio photograph taken in her thirties. During subsequent Kansas City visits at his duplex he shared several of his family photo albums. While identifying pictures of family members he came to one small child he said he couldn't identify.

"I don't know *who* that is," he said, appearing puzzled.

I was shocked seeing the five- or six-year-old child with the wide smile and brown sweater.

"That's me!"

"That's you?" he inquired, looking bewildered. "No, it can't be."

"That's me, that's my first-grade picture," I explained.

And obviously I knew from whom he had received the photo, but of course I had no idea when.

I always enjoyed talking with Myron. Not only for information I learned but for the sheer joy of conversation. Our conversations could be lively, thought provoking, or stimulating as well as challenging, uncompromising, and sometimes offensive.

It was clear that Myron danced to the beat of a different drummer, which could be positive or negative. I also discovered that he could be difficult to get along with. Myron let you know where he stood and where you stood with him. You knew how he felt; he did not hide his feelings or why he felt that way. Myron was not one to bite his tongue in order to be politically correct.

Myron told me that one of his daughters, who lived in California, resented him for not being a part of her life during her childhood and teen years. For many years he didn't know where she was. Regardless of her hurt and pain he was clear in his position. "She's over 21. She's grown. She should just get over it."

Sometimes he and I didn't agree. I saw the hardnosed, stubborn side of him that he maintained throughout his life.

In his later years, he was in conflict with some of his other children. It had been years since he had spoken to his third eldest son, George, named after his grandfather. George was a child from his marriage with Hurelene. Myron had ideas about the cause but he didn't make any attempts to find compromise.

George roomed for a time with his older brother Myron III, and Myron said that George's relations with him had also deteriorated to anger, hostility, and bitterness.

"You Black m* f*, you're going to wish you were dead," he recalled being told. Myron said Myron III was telling others in the community that he was already dead. Myron said the relationship really started to deteriorate after Hurelene's death in 1999. As with other disputes sometimes Myron would offer his thoughts as to possible reasons for the split, but, consistent with his personality, he did not seem to consider his son's perspective. Things were so tense with some of his children that Myron did not want them to be informed of his death.

"I don't understand why they treat me like they do," Myron would say. "I know I haven't done anything to them." Myron claimed that his estrangement from his children didn't bother him, but from his stressed facial expressions and pained eyes I thought otherwise.

In the short time that I knew Myron I could see where he could be controlling and domineering, which he admitted at least once. He desired to control as many aspects of his life as he could, and although he didn't verbalize it, that included people.

He told the story that after one of their divorces he found out Hurelene was dating again. Armed with a pistol, Myron hid in bushes near her residence not intending to harm Hurelene but to hurt her would-be suitor. Although he had the opportunity, Myron realized the error of his thinking and aborted his disastrous plan.

Hearing how he tried to influence people in minor situations, I could only imagine how he would have attempted to control major issues. And clearly that would not sit well with grown folk, including and especially his grown children. I came to understand why his relationships with some of his children were negative or nonexistent. I realized this was another possible reason Wanda might have attempted to keep us apart.

Myron's relations with most of his children seemed to range from neutral and fair to polite and cordial, and his relationship with a few appeared to be warm and harmonious, i.e. fatherly. The eldest daughter, Phyllis, maintained close contact with Myron across the years and visited from California from time to time. They first met at her high school graduation.

Myron noted that it took time, and children, for him to realize the most important aspects of life were far from the streets. "I found out what love was with Ebony," Myron said about his youngest daughter. He reminisced about his joy holding and rocking her when she was a small child. In her softness and innocence and vulnerability he experienced unconditional love. Myron finally felt, I believe, like a father.

Although Ebony moved with her mother from Kansas City to California as a child, Myron said he was always involved in her life. Even across the miles the relationship they established endured.

Myron said that he seldom drank; a six pack of beer would last for "a year." He didn't do drugs and refused to be in the company of people who did. When I saw photos of Myron with a joint in hand, he explained it as a dare and he did not inhale. Another photo showed him holding a shot glass in his hand.

What Myron said and what he actually did, in some instances seemed complex and sometimes contradictory. This man I came to know had a rather unique view of the world and of people. He could alienate or isolate people, shut them out, cut them off, dig emotional trenches between them and him, close his defensive gates, and shut down. Myron's perception of reality appeared crystal clear sometimes and at other times slightly skewed and quite different from others' perceptions. Sometimes his perception of the truth was not entirely accurate or realistic. Those misconceptions of course extended to close relatives.

My maternal grandmother Rosie Lee had been instrumental in my adoption by extended family. Rosie Lee was a strong-willed, insightful dynamo who protected her own, at any cost. It was Rosie Lee who intentionally and purposely kept Myron out of the loop regarding what happened with me as a baby. While Myron admitted to being a troubled teen, he did not recognize that his behavior did not endear him whatsoever to Rosie Lee.

In one conversation Myron and I talked of Rosie Lee. He mentioned that he attempted to see her during her last days in the hospital, but she died before he could make it as he had been incarcerated in juvenile detention. He was convinced that she had died a year earlier than she actually died. When I corrected him, he was puzzled and couldn't figure out why he didn't go see her. "She always kinda liked me," he said.

But Wanda noted to me years earlier that Rosie Lee warned her to stay away from Myron. "My mother told me to never have anything to do with that man. She never would tell me why."

The younger and middle-aged Myron was fashionable and "in" with the times. He was a cool, slick, lean, trim, and dapper dude, dressed to the nines, hair neatly trimmed in an Afro. He wore glasses or shades, a ring on his pinky finger, and a wide, expressive grin. He held an ever-present cigarette between his fingers. Until the day he died he drove Cadillacs. There are a number of photos of his favorite rides, an El Dorado, Sedan, Coupe De Ville, or Fleetwood. Even glancing through photos it's evident, from his body language, facial expressions, manner of dress, that Myron was not a man who suffered fools or a person to provoke.

But the man I knew in the latter years of his life was a homebody, someone who didn't socialize much with people, and who had given up the streets long years ago. Content to watch television, collect photographs, or fiddle on the computer, in some ways he had mellowed. It was this Myron who I found reflective, inquisitive, complimentary, and considerate. And he always asked how "Nana" (Wanda) was doing.

"Is there any word about Nana?"

Many times Myron said that Wanda was not only his first love, but the love of his life. Out of all the women and relationships in his life, Wanda stood alone, front and center. Of all the women he was involved with, Myron's mother held my birth mother in her highest regard. The one who got away.

Myron Clay in his Kansas City home office

Myron in his home with Reggie and Regina

Canetha, Regina, and I once visited with him in his duplex. Sitting at his dining room table late one quiet evening, his hair pulled back in his trademark ponytail, clothed again in dark slacks and sports shirt, moisture glistening in his eyes, Myron turned contemplative.

"You are what I always wanted to be" he said softly, proudly.

Although I don't recall all of the words he said to me, I remember his emotion and my feelings. He had hoped and prayed that we would someday meet and get to know each other. His prayers and mine were answered.

To God be the glory!

Although Myron hadn't attended church in years he emphasized he was a praying man. One of his grandmothers, who could be described as a prayer warrior, had left a lasting impression on him. Once, as a young man, Myron was badly burned after an outing on a boat in a Kansas City park. He didn't explain the details; I don't think he actually remembered. The prognosis was grim and he was near death. Myron remembers his grandmother being at his bedside, praying. He survived and remembered the power of her prayer, appreciative of his grandmother's faith and persistence in prayer.

I once asked Myron if he believed in Jesus Christ. He didn't answer my question directly, smoothly averting his answer to stating his strong belief in God. Aware of the basic theology of Seventh Day Adventists I was not surprised. I chose not to slip into lawyer mode and did not persist trying to get a direct answer to my question. He knew what I was asking, I knew what he was saying, and I let it go and never addressed it. It was not the appropriate time and although I did not bring it up again, later I believed I should have. He knew my beliefs, but perhaps I could have said something that might have given him something else to consider, if he was not a believer in Jesus as the Christ. Perhaps something I might have said could have caused a change in his mind and heart. Myron was a man who not only questioned but was also a deep, serious, critical thinker.

Life is full of "could have" moments. Essentially either one takes action or does not. Despite the analyzing, rationalizing, and justifying, I didn't take action, and that's on me. I still have hope, based on my beliefs, that when Myron went to his final slumber, he had made peace with God and accepted Jesus Christ as Lord and Savior.

The Myron I knew never withheld compliments, praise or encouragement. He was proud of my three children and definitely formed a connection with Regina. It was clear he was the source of several aspects of Regina's personality: from her quick, spontaneous witty quips to her creative, imaginative thinking.

Myron was also there to help in the ways he could, unselfish and considerate, even if it was to his own economic disadvantage. Myron had become computer savvy and he had a best friend who refurbished computers. Myron arranged for his friend to provide laptops, at cost, to several people, including us. Three laptops, one each to Regina, Canetha and myself, all surprise gifts, and greatly appreciated. Each time a computer needed to be maintained, updated, or repaired, we were to contact his friend and Myron took care of it. There even was a time that Regina's laptop needed to be replaced, and Myron had the second laptop sent to her new home in New York City. Myron's friend was a blessing to our family and we will forever be grateful to both Myron and his friend for their kindness. I started this book on the laptop Myron had sent to me when I was in seminary in California.

Thanks once again Myron!

I only took one car ride with Myron, and I was the driver. He was having some licensing problems with his Cadillac and was cautious about driving. I didn't mind driving my car, although I'd hoped to ride with him. It wasn't the car I was interested in, it was Myron as a driver. Of course, I didn't know this would be the first and only time we'd ride together.

Canetha and I were in Kansas City on a brief weekend trip when I asked Myron if he knew where Rosie Lee was buried. Myron knew exactly where and offered to show us. We made plans to go to the cemetery together the next day.

Beams of bright sunlight, clear blue skies, and mild temperatures embraced us the next day. Myron, riding shot gun, directed us to a Kansas City cemetery in the inner city. We parked and walked across the street. Myron's slow, measured stride and his shortness of breath required him to pause often despite the short distance. Clearly he had some major health issues, but they wouldn't deter him from his mission. Up a handful of concrete steps and a few steps from the cemetery sidewalk was Rosie Lee's final resting place.

After all these years, in a way I finally met my grandmother.

It took my biological father to show me. I reflected for a while — Myron was very patient — and then off we went for more glimpses of his past.

Myron directed me to where he thought the Catholic facility was in which I was born, but, to his astonishment, the building no longer existed. Instead, there were modern structures. It had been years since Myron had visited this part of central Kansas City.

There was another place he wanted to show us.

It was a short, rather direct drive to his boyhood home on Norton and he had no trouble guiding us there. His house was still standing. He pointed out some of the changes made to the structure of the two-story house. It was in fairly good condition, but not what I had envisioned. He had sold the house long ago.

Peace and resolution shone in Myron's eyes as he relished memories of days gone by.

"Back there," indicating the rear of the home, "is where my mother took care of people. We added that on," he explained, pointing to a room addition to the main house.

As with the cemetery, I couldn't help imagining life in this neighborhood, in his house, many decades ago.

As I drove off, Myron thought we were leaving, but I wasn't ready quite yet. I turned the car around and went back to the house for another look and pulled next to the curb. I did not want to rush this moment, appreciating still another piece to my life's puzzle.

Well, well, what do you know? So this is it.

My curiosity satisfied, we drove back to his duplex. He had offered to take us to the Ford plant where he had worked, but I suggested we do that another time. I thought we had time. Unfortunately, it never happened.

We dropped Myron off, said our goodbyes, and he lumbered slowly into his home. It was a wonderful visit, a good, productive day, crammed with lifetime memories from Myron's past. I believe he enjoyed this outing as much as I did, the opportunity to unravel layers of deeply buried experiences. While it was the first and only time we had shared such an experience, the important thing is that it happened. Not only did I have actual physical locations to go with the many stories, I got closer to my biological father. This Sunday morning drive revealed more roots to my ever expanding family tree.

CHAPTER 15
A Father's (Myron) Death

My phone vibrating, on a warm, Saturday evening, was very unusual. Although I was browsing in a hobby store with my wife, I chose to check the caller identification.

"Oh, it's Myron," I thought as I answered the call.

But to my great surprise it wasn't my biological father but his longtime partner of twenty-some years, Marilyn, with shocking news.

"Myron is under hospice care," she said. "He was released from the hospital earlier this morning."

My mind went blank, my body, numb and frozen in shock. I felt suspended from consciousness, physically here but mentally, spiritually, and emotionally disconnected from myself. Hospice care meant nearing death but this seemed so sudden.

Myron had been transported via ambulance from the hospital to their side-by-side duplex. He had been in the hospital since Sunday, July 7th, and the doctors weren't giving him much time to live, perhaps a week or two. Marilyn sensed he might not have that much time. And she was concerned about Myron's death instructions that he'd shared with some of us a year or so earlier.

"Myron wanted me to do all this stuff but didn't leave any money to do it with!" Her voice was anxious if not frantic. She was already talking about Myron in the past tense. I was still trying to process her words.

I had no idea that he'd been hospitalized (apparently Myron didn't want many people, including those of his children that he was on good terms, to know). And I certainly didn't know the serious health issues he'd suffered from for several months were now *killing* him. In our phone conversations I'd ask how he was feeling. Sometimes he would disclose how he was feeling, but even if it was something serious, he made light of the situation.

Now, during this July 13th conversation with Marilyn, she needed comfort and reassurance. Inner family hostility and conflict dictated that she be extremely careful now that Myron was vulnerable.

Marilyn was looking for specific advice, and I needed some time to collect my thoughts. Standing in the middle aisle of a retail specialty store was not the place. I also wondered if Marilyn was also looking for money. Unfortunately, I had absolutely nothing to offer her.

"I'm not home now but I'll call you back," I promised, providing time to return home and gather my thoughts. I recalled what would be our last phone conversation, on Father's Day, 2013. Like many of our latter phone conversations, this one was rather brief. Perhaps less than five minutes. Our extended, hour-plus-long conversations had ceased long ago.

In the four years since our first meeting in 2009 we had been getting to know each other; now we were secure, comfortable, and appreciative of our very late in life relationship. We had been given the opportunity to get to *know* each other.

But that last conversation was unique, not so much because of what was said but because of what it was: a final conversation between a father and son, on a Father's Day, a conversation decades in the making. Our conversation did not climax in words of love spoken but our love declared itself in the action of making the connection.

"How are you doing?" I questioned.

"How you be Mr. Reggie?!" was Myron's response.

"How are you feeling these days?"

"I'm still kicking," Myron countered, "just not as high."

Myron just didn't sound like Myron. He didn't complain of many, if any, ailments, but his voice just did not sound as strong as usual, and I made a mental note of it. While his voice wasn't hoarse or muffled, it was much weaker than usual. No longer vibrant, the power and strength in his timbre and tone were missing.

A year or so before this he'd had some sick spells and had been hospitalized. By the time I was told, his life had returned to normal. His voice again his strong, deep, uniquely Myron bass. Nothing even slightly hinted this would be my last conversation with the man I'd spent years wondering about and visualizing.

It was Father's Day and Myron had no special holiday plans. He was just taking it easy, doing "not much of nothing." In fact, that's how he spent much of his time after retiring from the Kansas City Ford plant after 35-some years, doing much of nothing. And that was fine with him.

"I haven't been out of the house for two weeks or more," he'd often say. Unless he had errands, a doctor's appointment, or something he deemed vital, Myron was content to spend his time on his computer in that small office he'd made from a spare bedroom. Or watching television. His was a sedentary existence with little to no physical activity.

His relaxed attitude extended to the very basics.

"Some days I don't get dressed," Myron admitted. "For what? I'm not going anywhere." That was his explanation for sitting around his duplex all day in his underwear shorts (generally without t-shirt).

That last phone conversation was just bits and pieces of this and that, no outstanding revelations about life, family, or himself. Our earlier conversations had helped me understand more about his life, his family, his thoughts, and philosophy. They had helped me understand who I was and where I came from as I learned from him about my previously unknown and unexplored family branch.

This Father's Day conversation wasn't notable in any way. Except being our last.

We made small talk and that was it. Myron didn't mention if any of his eight other biological children had phoned or the three others that he had adopted.

I can't remember who closed this conversation but it was most likely Myron. He didn't want to keep me but always expressed his gratitude for any phone call. This time was no different.

"Thank you for calling" (sometimes he would add, "the old man").
"I just wanted to wish you a happy Father's Day. You take care," I said.
"Goodbye."

Did he say *Bye* that last time? Curious how something as usual and mundane as a simple goodbye can become a big deal in retrospect.

That was it. It was over. Our physical, earthly relationship had run its course, a relationship of more than fifty years that, despite being concentrated in four years (2009–2013), finally made me feel *whole.* I felt an urge to call Myron on July 4th but didn't.

"I just called him on Father's Day," I rationalized. "I'll call some other time." It wasn't that I was waiting for him to call; he had done so on occasion. I just simply did not call.

I collected my thoughts and phoned Marilyn later that Saturday, July 13th. Myron was bedridden but conscious, able to understand or talk. Clearly he knew what was going on, what was happening, and what was going to happen. Myron had been in failing health for several weeks. A dear friend of his who saw him after July 4th had urged him to go to a hospital. Initially rejecting the suggestion, Myron finally relented and suggested, on Sunday July 7th, that Marilyn get him to a hospital. He gave instructions that no one was to be contacted, apparently not wanting any visitors. During the early morning hours of July 12th Myron was released and sent home via ambulance. His last ride home.

After my second conversation with Marilyn, I prayed and meditated. *Should I go to Kansas City? When?* I decided to travel to Kansas City Sunday morning and return to Wichita that night and called a rental car company. Monday morning I had to be at my part time job and teach a class.

I watched the 10 p.m. local television weathercast for Sunday. It promised severe thunderstorms. Going to bed I had no trouble falling asleep. My plans were made.

B – O – O – M ! B – O – O – M !

Early Sunday morning, July 14th, despite an eye mask and ear plugs, sounds of loud thunder, like gigantic boulders falling just outside my window, shook me from a sound sleep.

Thunder or lightening rarely wake me. They don't bother me because I remember what Wanda often said about the weather: "That's God's business. I just have to deal with it."

Looking through the closed window blinds, I saw no rain, no wind, no lightning. I thought that unusual.

B – O – O – M! B – O – O – M !

Again loud claps of thunder. Nothing else.

I became restless. It was about 3:00 a.m. and I couldn't fall back to sleep. Tossing, turning, restless, I was not at peace. I felt what soul singer James Brown sang in the 1960's hit "Cold Sweat." Despite my tight schedule and very limited resources, I wanted to see Myron one last time. I'd not seen him since the summer of 2011. I'd relocated from California to Wichita in 2012 and money was tight, even for a rental car.

More claps of thunder, then the patter of raindrops. For logistical reasons this trip would be challenging.

Again I prayed. *Should I go? Is this a sign?*
Then I realized the answer. No. Not this trip, not this time.

And I remembered something from the very beginning in my search for Myron. It was always about timing — when to search, when to write, when to call, when to follow up — timing was always essential.

I heeded the signs, changed my plans, and canceled the car rental. I was at peace. With everything. With Myron. I decided to go to the YMCA, but it didn't open until 6:30 a.m.

Between 5 a.m. and 6:15 a.m., I was up and wide awake. Usually in the wee hours of the night I pray, read the Bible, or just piddle around. But that morning I just can't recall what I was doing. Everything was a blur and I was in an emotional fog.

I went to the downtown YMCA and stuck to my routine, lifting weights for 10-15 minutes followed by cardio (either bicycling or the treadmill). I had my phone in my gym bag but didn't check it until I arrived back home.

Before leaving for church, I checked my phone. Marilyn had called about 7:30 a.m., an hour earlier. I called.

The news really didn't surprise me.

"Myron died this morning" she said. About 5:20 a.m. he called her.

"Tootsie! Ice!" He wanted some ice to swallow.

She went to him.

Myron was a shell of the solid, stocky man he once was. Congestive heart failure, diabetes and a lifetime of smoking had taken its toll. Lying in a hospital bed Myron gazed at his companion of twenty-some years.

"Don't worry" he said, "everything is going to be all right."
Then Myron took his last breath and fell asleep to eternity. It was over.

My wife and I attended a 9:40 a.m. worship service at a Methodist Church, but I made no announcement about my father. Although we often attended the church, we were not members. Even after more than a year, few people knew our names.

I called Marilyn later that evening and we talked more about her plans. She wanted to leave Kansas City as soon as possible.

Monday morning I went to work as usual. I was teaching as an adjunct general education teacher at Wichita Technical College. My supervisor said someone would fill in if I needed to leave town. We spoke of Myron very briefly. I taught my interpersonal communications class. Life went on, as usual.

I talked to Marilyn once or twice that week. Myron had long before informed us that he wanted to be cremated with no funeral, no memorial, no grave site service. And he didn't want some of his other children to be informed. Not only had there been little to no communication with them in the past few years, but when I had asked him if there was any chance of reconciliation, he had predicted "none." There had been harsh treatment and violent threats.

Consequently, some children, even at his death, were never told about the other child of his, a child born to a fourteen-year-old mother whom Myron frequently referred to as the "love of his life." A child who had made Myron a first-time father at age sixteen. Me.

Fifty years in the making, fifty years of questions, and finally meeting when I was more than fifty years old.

More than once he'd mentioned his concern for the reaction of some of my siblings if he told them of me. So he didn't. Ever.

Upon Myron's death there were no heartbreaking goodbyes, no emotional, celebratory homegoing services, no funeral program, no newspaper obituary, no freshly cut, arranged, scented flowers, no death announcement — just ashes in an urn transported to his chosen place of rest, somewhere in Louisiana.

Just like he wanted.

I often think of Myron — how can I not? One lasting memory of the man who usually held his emotions in check happened during a visit to his duplex. He said something that I will always hold dear: "You are what I'd hoped to be." Tears welled in his eyes.

Myron is permanently etched in the hearts of those that he loved and in those who loved him, he still lives.

Myron was my father. And I am, in part, Myron.

"Mr. Reggie, how you be?!"

Myron in his home

CHAPTER 16: EPILOGUE
Nanny's Peace

Nanny/Wanda was a different person when I graduated from the seminary. When I started in 2008, she had recovered from her first stroke and was back to being "herself"; when I finished she was confined to her bed, miserable, patiently waiting for her change.

It was the fourth Sunday in September 2016 when peace finally came. The prior week medical caregivers had informed the family Wanda's time with us was nearing an end. Thus family and friends gathered in her home around her bedside that last Sunday afternoon. There were twelve of us that encircled her bedside, from the oldest family member, an 80-something-year-old aunt, one of Red Boy's surviving sisters, to the youngest, sister Tina's 30-something daughter Danielle. Wanda's eyes were open, she was conscious, and seemed very aware of our presence and what was going on. She was in the moment.

"It's all right Momma. Go to your peace," Tina reassured our mother. Then it was one high spiritual moment after another. A moment of transition, but also of peace. A moment of sadness but also of joy.

Nanny's brother, Red Boy's son Curtis Jones, Jr. offered a heartfelt, stirring prayer of praise, hope and thanksgiving. Sister Erika's husband, Pastor Clayborn Jones, started the song, "Pass Me Not" with all of us joining in.

Pass me not O gentle Savior, hear my humble cry.
while on others thou are calling, do not pass me by.
Savior, Savior, hear my humble cry,
while on others thou are calling,
do not pass me by.

Sometime during the singing, Nanny slipped from our present into the eternal. She went from the temporal presence of physical family and friends into the eternal spiritual company of all of the family, the ancestors known and unknown. She became one of the great cloud of witnesses as she walked into the arms of Jesus. It was a beautiful, loving homegoing. Wanda was free from her bondage, her pain, her misery.

I was reminded of that old African American/Negro spiritual Dr. Martin Luther King sometimes quoted: "Free at last, free at last, thank God almighty I'm free at last!"

I gave my Nanny, my loving mother Wanda, a final kiss and closed her eyes. I wept.

Several hours later, about 9:00 p.m. or so, the morticians were removing Nanny from her long-time home. The night was dark, the air was still, stars twinkled brightly in the fall sky.

Ding, ding, ding!
Ding, ding, ding!

What do you know? I thought to myself, astonished as to what I heard.

Just as we were following our Nanny's body to the hearse, in the background, from a neighborhood church, church bells were ringing! Never in my life of visiting her home over the course of forty-some years had I ever heard church bells ringing. I imagined the bells were just for Wanda, and perhaps for us, a sign, a miracle, perhaps a welcome home. Or maybe they were for us, a glorious conclusion to a life well lived. A message that everything was all right, that she was all right.

As she requested, I preached her funeral. After years of suffering, Wanda Louise McClain Grant was whole again, young again. After those long hard years of misery, my dear Nanny was finally at rest. I reminded the congregation during her funeral, she was

Free at last, free at last!
Thank God almighty Nanny is free at last!

Wanda McClain Grant

The End

ABOUT THE AUTHOR

Reginald D. Jarrell has taught at Southwestern College, Winfield, Kansas; St. Ambrose University, Davenport, Iowa; Southern University in New Orleans, Louisiana; Alcorn State University, Lorman, Mississippi; and at two community colleges in Iowa and Illinois. His legal experience includes work as assistant public defender, Rock Island County, Illinois, and staff attorney, Prairie State Legal Services, Rock Island. His communications experience includes working as television production staff, Family Radio, Oakland, California; as a newspaper staff reporter for The Moline Publishing Company, Moline, Illinois; and as a television news reporter, WHO- TV, Des Moines, Iowa. He has also worked as a janitor and a shoe salesperson.

He earned a Juris Doctor degree, University of Iowa Collegeof Law, Iowa City, Iowa; a Master of Divinity, American Baptist Seminary of the West, Berkeley, California; a Master of Science, Mass Communication and Journalism, Iowa State University, Ames, Iowa; a Bachelor of Arts in Communication, The American University, Washington, D.C.; and a Doctor of Ministry degree from The Berkeley School of Theology, formerly American Baptist Seminary of the West.

Jarrell's writing includes a book of essays, *31 Days (Nights): Memoir of Living Black in America* (Blue Cedar Press, 2022), *Wings* (a children's book), and television/film screenplays. He enjoys reading, film, theater, travel, and current events.

Jarrell's family consists of wife Canetha, two sons, one daughter, six grandchildren, and one small dog. Jarrell has lived in several places across the United States and currently resides in south central Kansas.